Work in Progress...

The Toolbox for the Job

Mary Barrett

iUniverse, Inc.
New York   Bloomington

iUniverse books may be ordered through booksellers or by contacting:

iUniverse
1663 Liberty Drive
Bloomington, IN 47403
www.iuniverse.com
1-800-Authors (1-800-288-4677)

Because of the dynamic nature of the Internet, any Web addresses or
links contained in this book may have changed since publication and
may no longer be valid. The views expressed in this work are solely those
of the author and do not necessarily reflect the views of the publisher,
and the publisher hereby disclaims any responsibility for them.

ISBN: 978-1-4502-2306-5 (sc)
ISBN: 978-1-4502-2307-2 (ebook)

Printed in the United States of America

iUniverse rev. date: 4/5/2010

Dedication

This book, first and above all, is dedicated to the continued glory and honor of God. It is by the use of His tools that we are equipped for the journey of life. May we all be good stewards of what we are entrusted with, fully understanding how to use the gifts His hand had supplied.

Table of Contents

Dedication   v

Invitation   ix

Introduction   xv

Chapter One: Using the Tool of Acting on Salvation   1

Chapter Two: Using the Tool of the Bible   12

Chapter Three: Using the Tool of Forgiveness   25

Chapter Four: Using the Tool of Baptism   40

Chapter Five: Using the Tool of a
Community of Believers   52

Chapter Six: Using the Tool of Faith   67

Chapter Seven: Using the Tool of Serving   81

Chapter Eight: Using the Tool of Your Witness   95

Chapter Nine: Using the Tool of
Tithes and Offerings   107

Chapter Ten: Using the Tool of Fasting   118

Afterwards   133

About the Author   139

Invitation

If you are like me (or probably like most women,) you rarely give any thought to the importance of tools. What is it about a tool that makes them so appealing to the average man? What is it that causes husbands to get up early on a Saturday morning for a sale at Home Depot or Lowe's; but, somehow find it impossible to get up to help with the morning feedings of the baby? Do they really need so many intimidating-looking tools filling the garage until it is practically bulging at the seams?

I can definitely appreciate the practicality of an old trusty screwdriver, the faithful hammer and the multipurpose duct tape; but, delve into any tool topic beyond those and you have lost my interest of engaging in mechanical conversation. During our 20 years of marriage I have posed these same questions to my husband, Tom. He always smiles and says, "Hon, it is all about having the right tool for the right job." In applying this idea to many aspects of life, I was surprised to find out how much wisdom and truth that statement contains. My eyes became open to the "right tools" as I searched scriptures and considered which stories to include in this discussion. Later on in this devotional study we will come back to that statement to apply it to other principles.

It is certainly not my intention to begin by offending my fellow women by insinuating that we are naïve when it comes to using tools. So, if you are a nuts-and-bolts type of gal, I say, "Way to go, sister!" In fact, I am proud to tell the story of my sister in law, who served with Habitat for Humanity faithfully for several years. She had many important roles on the crews she worked with and even spent time in Alaska helping on a project there. I believe that every construction site needs a pink hard hat or two – you just won't see one on me. To be perfectly honest, the only time I give tools a second thought is when I am griping at my husband to pick up after using his.

Even if power tools and the history of sanding blocks are not high on my list of conversation topics, I do acknowledge that nothing gets started or created without the use of good tools. Without them, a community can not be built, fixed, or reconstructed. Tools are a vital part of survival in all cultures and societies of the world. Is it a true statement to say; that without the knowledge and ability to effectively use tools properly, people would fail to thrive? Progress stops, innovation ceases, deterioration of structures goes unchecked, and the depilation of resources begins. It's hard to believe that investing in good tools can possibly prevent all of that, isn't it?

God already knows that if we do not have access to the tools we need in order to accomplish the task of working on and "fixing" ourselves, our journey here on earth will suffer the same fate that an abandoned structure does. To use a cliché, life happens. All of us, from time to time, will break down, get a little rusty, and even sometimes find ourselves in desperate need of an all-over makeover. People depend on tools to supplement their creativity and construct strong, reliable resources to properly and effectively apply to their lives. Those who choose not to keep a toolbox full of useful equipment to maintain a healthy well-being in body, mind and soul, will in time, no longer be viable but often find their energy weakening. It is the job of the Holy Spirit to help support and guide us in building our lives on the work that God wants us to do. The work Christ began is now ours to continue. As we read about what Jesus has done, we will gather for ourselves each tool of the Christian trade and place it our own toolbox to use in completing the job of living a Spirit-filled life pleasing to God.

For some, the concept of rolling up our sleeves, putting on a hard hat and strapping on a tool belt may be an unfamiliar idea. If that is the case for you, please do not be discouraged; there are new things just ahead that will build up your relationship with Jesus and encourage you to continue to grow more and more on your spiritual journey. Do you have a heart that desires to pick up those tools designed by God to transform your life, potentially rubbing off on those around you? Then you are invited to join us on this heaven-bound construction site!

The blueprints have already been drawn and are laid out for us in God's Holy Word, the Bible. That is the first and most important tool you are required to learn to use before we proceed. The Bible is invaluable in determining how effectively we will perform our tasks we face. Together we are going to read and learn what God's master plan is. We will also pray and ask God to make that plan come alive and to become real for us to experience personally. If you are ready to accept that challenge, then let's begin the journey. Don't worry if you are starting from what seems like an empty place; I promise that if you listen for God's guidance and follow the directions of the Holy Spirit, you will be filled to overflowing with the confidence and focus you need. In Deuteronomy 6:3 we read, "Listen closely… to everything I say. Be careful to obey. Then all will go well with you." Can we all realize this? If we listen to God's Word and apply it to our lives, the promise is that we will be blessed.

This is the fourth book in the Mother in Love devotional study series. We began this series with exploring the understanding that God has already placed everything good in our lives with the fruit of the Holy Spirit. Next we moved on to going back and remembering that Jesus ought to be the first love of our lives always. Then, once we accepted the fruit of the Spirit and the love of Christ, our only response is to praise His Holy name and call out to Him in prayer. Now we are getting ready to take the next leap, my friends, out into deeper water and greater commitment to the Lord. We have reached the part of our walk where our words and actions must match. In these reflections, we are going to explore why we need to use all the tangible gifts supplied to us by God as our tools in our journey. Doing this will strengthen our relationship with Him and be a good reflection in helping others get there too.

Are you ready to encounter the 10 tools to be used and placed in your eternal toolbox? Be warned; this requires more then reading the Bible. The process stems from there, but must also turn into action. In this book, we will develop a plan to both read and apply God's Word into our daily Christ-centered walk. Not only are we going to discover the things that God says we should be doing; but, we are also actually going to try to do them ourselves aided by the tools we need for each job. This is why I believe God wants us to be active participants with Him; He is the one who gave these gifts to the church – the apostles, the prophets, the evangelists, the pastors, and the teachers. Their responsibility is to equip God's people to do this work and build up the church, the body of Christ... (Ephesians 4:11-12). We are that body of Christ; therefore, we are called to be united with all the other parts of that body.

There we have it, God wants to expose each one of us to the truth, so that, we may be equipped for the job of living every day in this imperfect world as it stands now until the glory of Jesus returns. Can we work hard, love God more each day and commit to using all of our rich resources found in Christ? Through God's Word we have more available to us than mere mirages of stories, fairy tales, myths or suggestions about God. Let's read these words of Scripture. Take them into our hearts and prepare to get busy and focus on contributing to a better world, beginning by looking closely at ourselves.

2 Timothy 3:16-17

"All Scripture is inspired by God and is useful to teach us what is wrong in our lives. It straightens us out and teaches us to do what is right. It is God's way of preparing us in every way, fully equipped for every good thing God wants us to do.

May we all be quipped and able to do what God asks us to do!

* The Biblical references made throughout this book are taken from the New Living Translation (NLT) version, unless specified otherwise.

Introduction

It is easy to call ourselves Christians, but if the characteristics of a Christian are not understood, there can be a false sense of righteousness gained simply because we may think that all we need to do is show up, take up space in a pew on Sunday mornings and hand an envelope in with a check enclosed. If that is all we believe is needed, then we have missed the mark and there is work to do. This may be a tough confrontation; but, please stay with me as I ask this question: isn't it time for those who claim the title of Christian to stop "playing church?" Week after week, people return home from worship with the habit of forgetting and not applying the message they have just heard or perhaps they remember it until they get back into their routine Monday through Saturday. Christianity is not about putting God on like a coat and taking Him off when it is convenient. When we attempt to move away from God, it is impossible for us to live in the Light of the Lord. God wants to be close to us so He can dwell inside each one of us (refer to 1 Corinthians 6:19-20). He designed us and the world that way on purpose.

Romans 8:9 presents this thought-provoking statement, "You are controlled by the Spirit if you have the Spirit of God living in you." Knowing that, how can

God ever not dwell where we are or not be involved in our lives, no matter what the day? And remember that those who do not have the Spirit of Christ living in them cannot be Christians at all. The only way a Christian life is possible is if a person is in direct partnership with the Spirit of Christ. The theme carried throughout this devotional study is that our relationship with God needs to be lived from the inside out with a whole heart. We will be reading Scripture and applying principles that support the definition of what it is to live a Christian life, including both being chosen by God and following Jesus Christ.

The Mother in Love Series is designed to be an interactive and invitational way for you to explore what God wants to reveal in your life. Each devotional book has been based on a Spiritual principle. As the title suggests, our principle in this volume is gaining the tools that will enable us to fully live out a fruitful life during our time here on earth, because this physical time is a journey and process that is ever changing as we mature and grow spiritually. Throughout these pages, it is my prayer that two things will be conveyed clearly: first that we develop a deeper knowledge that being an authentic Christian is both believing in your heart and confessing that Jesus lived, died and rose again to reconcile us to the Father as our only Savior. Second, I hope we will learn that as a Christian we are children of God, chosen and set apart for service. We are to worship (as we learned in the third devotional of the Mother in Love Series) and witness to others by the means of the same invitation that was extended to us by Christ. Matthew 22:14 explains to us that many are called, but few are chosen and profit simply because they do not accept the invitation to come to the

Great Feast that is being prepared for us in heaven. Let those be blessed who have decided to utilize the tools of the Spirit which God has instructed us with or have not grown weary of the work when the job gets tough.

Mom's Message

The Mother in Love series was inspired by my mother-in-law, Betty, who modeled for me the beauty of a Christ-centered life. Through the 18 years of loving discipleship that she invested in me, my mother-in-law modeled each principle needed to live a life pleasing to the Lord. These particular devotions are intended to celebrate the joy of showing others the love of Christ through our testimonies. A favorite saying of Mom used to be, "Preach the Gospel at all times and, when necessary, use words" (Quote by St. Francis of Assisi).

Each book so far in the series has begun with a personal moment with mom where I experienced the principle being applied that we will discuss in the devotionals. The Mother in Love devotionals have been built upon five concepts of an authentic Christian life. This book puts God's Word into action, so it is tough to tell just one story in this case.

So, I have decided to share with you Mom's main message to me and what her first call to action was to me when I first became a Christian. She knew that some elements were going to be crucial to my survival as a new born-again believer in Jesus. Mom was quick on the task of arming me with the ammunition I needed to fuel my Christian walk. Right away she gave me my very own Bible, placed my children and me in our first church "family," and wasted little time taking me to every Bible study and women's event she could find. Those are some of the important tools we are going to discuss. I am so grateful that Mom took part in equipping me so well to work as partner on the Lord's team.

In addition to all the tools she physically gave to me, the words of Scripture that she repeated have stuck with me. She told me that all I need to believe as a Christian is contained in Acts 2:38, and what Christians are to become involved with was written out in Acts 2:42 & 47. I was nervous after I accepted Jesus into my heart. Even though my mother-in-law was there to edify me, I didn't know if I could stay strong on my journey. What a change Jesus makes in your world! But despite my feeling overwhelmed, her example and message using the words of the apostle Peter encouraged me. I witnessed these scriptures she shared with me become relevant and alive. Peter said, "Each one of you must turn away from your sins and be baptized in the name of Jesus Christ, so that your sins will be forgiven; and you will receive God's gift, the Holy Spirit." The disciples of the day spent their time learning from the apostles, taking part in fellowship, and sharing in the fellowship of meals and prayers... praising God and enjoying the good will of all people... (Acts 2:38-42 & 47, The Good News Version of the Bible)

Remember that it is only when we use the tools that the Lord has given us can we do the work He has chosen us to do.

Format of Devotions

At the conclusion of each chapter there is a section to

draw you into God's Word, called Questions to Consider. Set time apart each day to let the Holy Spirit search your heart as you answer the questions that will encourage you to use the tools God has designed for you. This is a good exercise to do with a small group or during quiet personal reflection. After you have finished with the questions, you can move on to the section entitled The Tool of Scripture. In this portion, more detailed scripture is offered that pertains to the topic you have read. If you wish to go further into the message, meditate on God's Word that has been given and try writing out the verses that have been referenced. The blank pages after the chapter, titled What's in My Toolbox, are provided for you to track any insight or thoughts you might have experienced and to answer any questions that you find meaningful.

A practice that has become a useful tool for me is journaling. The moments when the Holy Spirit teaches our hearts are precious and should be recorded. Located in the back of the book you will find additional blank pages headed Things to Work On. Please record anything that has been revealed to you for later reference so that you can go back and track your personal growth.

Chapter One:

Using the Tool of Acting on Salvation

Building on the Word of God – 1 Corinthians 1:24 – But to those called by God to salvation, both Jews and Gentiles, Christ is the mighty power of God and the wonderful wisdom of God.

As the Scriptures say, "The person who wishes to boast should boast only of what the Lord has done."

Salvation is the mega tool that joins together our lives with that of Jesus Christ. Being united with Jesus radically reconstructs and reshapes everything that our lives once looked like. Why? Because His purpose is to exclusively destroy the dominion of sin in our lives, releasing us from strongholds and reconnecting us to the love of God. Salvation is based upon the atonement wrought by Christ for our wrongdoing. All men (and women) are freely offered this gift, but it cannot be received without repentance and faith in Christ from the heart. The work of salvation is to bring about the forgiveness, regeneration, sanctification, justification and reconciliation of all true believers. Our Christian walk starts here and can be built on nothing else but the solid rock and foundation of the salvation of Jesus. Backing up that statement are the words Jesus spoke that have been recorded for us in the Gospel of Matthew. Matthew 7:24 and 26-27 explain to us how this process works. "Anyone who listens to my teaching and obeys me is wise, like a person who builds a house on solid rock.... But anyone who hears my teaching and ignores it is foolish, like a person who builds a house on sand. When the rain and the floods come and the winds beat against that house, it will fall with a mighty crash." I hope those verses support the concept that what we build with and what we build our life upon matter greatly regarding the outcome we will experience.

All tools will come with instructions. If you are like my son, you throw the instruction sheet out, thinking you can figure out how to make it work correctly on your own. But as we become a little older and wiser, we value instructions and appreciate having them. Instructions hold the formulas we need to help accomplish what we want. We cannot just do it our own way and get the proper result. That is the same with God; we cannot live our lives without asking Him to be a part of it and expecting Him to be at work for our good. Let's think for a moment about the reasons instructions are included with the tools we use. I agree that the safety and efficiency of the tool are important, because we know that tools not used as intended can cause tragic results, but have you thought about the responsibility of the one who might intend to use the tool? Once the maker of that particular tool seals the box and has included every piece (even the directions) necessary, it no longer is his concern if it gets used properly or not. The person picking up that tool has the responsibility to gather the information and take the necessary precautions that will guarantee that the tool will perform safely and work the way it was designed to.

What do you suppose salvation was designed to do? I think if we recap the opening verse, it will help answer that question. Salvation is the tool used to call *all people* (of all faiths, from every nation of the world) to God for safety and spiritual mercies. What happens in us as the result of salvation is deliverance from eternal death, ease from bondages that tie us up here on earth and a soundness of mind that we are now relying on the one true God who hears our prayers. The action we must choose is to learn how to apply and take advantage of all these benefits. I have concluded that salvation is a two-part belief. God's word is presented in two parts, which are the Old and New Testament of the Bible. The prophesies describing the coming Messiah (the One who is to come, the Anointed Redeemer) are told in the books of the Old Testament, while the fulfillment of those promises are given to us in the New Testament accounts through the birth, life, death and resurrection of Jesus Christ who is that Messiah foretold to come and save His people. When we stay on one side of the story we do not see how marvelous the whole picture of God's plan for us is. As is the case in reading those instructions, our minds need to be open to the whole story. Every good story has a beginning, a middle and an end. We can not fully appreciate the story if parts are missing or if we refuse to move forward or hang on to the parts we are comfortable with. The best part about God's story is that we are all included in it and it has no end in sight. Do you have a chapter that you would like to write or possibly re-write? Salvation allows us to erase our mistakes and replace them with fresh changes! Is there anyone who would not want a second chance at life if it were offered? This information sums up simply that there is a second chance available and waiting for us. But again, it refers back to the opening verse of this chapter, which states that the spiritual rebirth and abundant life of the Holy Spirit and ultimately eternal life with our Creator all starts with what Jesus came into the world to do. It is His goodness poured on us that we rejoice in and share with others. Our only contribution is being the recipients of such a great love, leaving us nothing to brag about except what has been done for us. Therefore, it is that which Christ has done that we boast in and share through our stories from spiritual death to new life.

Anita's story:

We talked about the love of Christ and the act of salvation for all people – Jews and non-Jews. Without going into an extensive theological lesson, the Jewish people were the chosen ones of God and the apple of His eye (reference Psalm 105:37-45). Romans 3:2 explains that the Jewish people were entrusted with the whole revelation of God. These are the people to whom God wanted to send the Messiah, but because they thought righteousness could be accomplished on their own by following religious commandments; they rejected the message and their King who would save them. You can read this account and involve yourself in the love God extended to His people in the first five books of the Bible, called the Pentateuch. These are the writings of Moses and the account of the Jewish people's release from captivity and ultimate rebellion against God.

Although this account describes the Jewish people of that time, we all are stiffnecked people and often do not realize that we are living life in darkness without the light of Jesus and the friendship of God. Although it may be difficult to acknowledge this and change, but unless we do, we will never be free of all the burdens that weigh us down and rob us of having complete joy because we are missing the freedom of salvation.

Anita's illustrates perfectly the Scripture and the intention of this specific chapter. There are many parts to Anita's testimony, each part inspirational, but we will focus on her personal encounter with the knowledge of religion to her rebirth into a relationship with God. I find it truly amazing when the ones that God first called to be His people (Jews) turn back to Him. Anita is a dear lady I know from church and our women's weekly community group. She is very open to discuss her heart for the Lord because she is on fire with the love of Jesus – her Messiah. Her personality radiates that her life has been transformed by the gift of new life, and although she now is a Christian she appreciates even more the beauty of her Jewish faith. This was not always true in Anita's life. I will let Anita share with you, with her permission and in her own words, her story through an email she sent me. See if you can pick up on the ways she has acted on the tool of salvation that she now carries in her personal toolbox of resources from the Holy Spirit.

Dear Mary,
Just wanted to let you know I feel really honored that you even considered my testimony for your book. You are

absolutely right when you say that God has blessed my family. The best part is that He continues to bless us.

I would like to share with you how my life has changed amazingly over the past two years. I was raised in a Jewish household, as were both my sons. In November 2007, I was introduced to my son's friend, who started me on a journey to come to know our Lord and Savior, Jesus Christ. In June 2008, I started attending Keystone Community Fellowship [This is the church Anita and I both attend now] and was baptized in July. Within the next 9 months, both of my sons, my daughter-in-law and two grandchildren gave their lives to Jesus and were baptized at Keystone as well.

Prior to becoming acquainted with the Lord, I had many strongholds, including anxiety, trust issues and abandonment issues, all stemming from my father, who left us when I was 18. That caused me to feel like I always had to be in control of everything and everyone, including myself. Those strongholds led to two failed marriages and a life searching for fulfillment, which only led to disappointment over and over again.

Once I came to the Lord and left all my anxieties and fears at the foot of the cross, realizing that I am not in control of anything or anyone, including myself, my life rapidly changed. I no longer suffer from generalized anxiety disorder. Also, I no longer make any decisions without praying first. Most importantly, I wait for God's answer, which doesn't always come as quickly as I would like, but through faith, I am learning to wait.

Does this mean that my life is always a bed of roses? Not at all, but now even when I'm being attacked by worldly problems and I'm sad, I can still experience peace and joy through it all. I know this feeling of total peace and joy I now have can only come from the Holy Spirit within me.

I used to say that my life was like a book with the last chapter missing, but I've found that last chapter, and my life is now complete with my Lord, Jesus.

Found in the love of Christ,
Anita

I want to thank Anita for being so brave and transparent; being vulnerable is not always what feels natural. Anita spoke about how being in control gives us a sense of security that we all like, but, I can tell you that, if you are ready and give Jesus control of your heart, it will be the most secure you have ever felt. Jesus promises that one day we will be with Him in heaven forever. Check it out for yourself; take the time to read what Jesus says He is going to do in the gospel of John 14:1-4. If you want to claim that promise for yourself, I pray that you will consider salvation and act right now upon God's endless love. He is there, and your reservation is already made if you want it.

Questions to Consider

+ Have you experienced salvation? If yes, what does it look like for you? If not, are you able to identify what is holding you back?

+ Why is it we are told that we are living in spiritual darkness without salvation? Read John 8:12-20. Write out your thoughts.

+ If salvation cost God His only Son and Jesus His life, what does salvation cost you? Read John 3:16-17 and Romans 3:21-31.

+ Look at these verses from Romans 4:6-8 and make a list of the benefits experienced if we apply and use the tool and gift of salvation.

+ Based on everything we learned and read; why would you say salvation is the foundation of a Christian life?

The Tool of Scripture

Romans 3:9, Isaiah 41:14, Psalm 26, Daniel 12:3, Luke 2:25-32, John 16:33

Colossians 2:6-7 & 13-15, 1 Samuel 2:9-19, Proverbs 2:1-8, Acts 16:31

What's in My Toolbox

Chapter Two:

Using the Tool of the Bible

Building on the Word of God – Luke 24:44-45 – Then [Jesus] said to them, "These are the very things I told you about while I was still with you: everything written about me in the Law of Moses, the writings of the prophets, and Psalms had come true." Then he opened their minds to the understanding of the Scriptures.

One day our daughter Montana came home from school excited to tell me everything about a boy who was new to her school. She knew his name, where he previously lived, the color of his hair and eyes, and even some of the things he liked and doesn't like. What made her able to repeat all this? It was because Montana took the time to ask questions so that she could know him better. Although she could describe her friend to me, I did not share in the personal experience of meeting him myself. You really cannot say that you know someone until you meet them. We can be given names, facts and general information about a person and be familiar with those facts; but, it is not until we meet him or her ourselves that we really begin to know the heart of a person. As Montana continued to relay all the information she had found out about her recent acquaintance, it occurred to me that we are drawn to get to know someone who intrigues us. Most people won't exert the energy unless they find something valuable or worthy of the investment of time. It takes effort and dialogue to get to know more than someone's name; we must be willing to become involved with him or her if we are truly interested in knowing that person.

My husband currently has the task of teaching our middle daughter how to drive. Tom and Jessica come home with some great (and some scary!) stories of their roadway adventures. They are quite real to them, but they are just stories to me. As much as I love and can relate to what they retell, I didn't experience the stories for myself. The point is, unless a story or event is personally experienced, there is always a part of the story that keeps others just on the outside.

I think the two examples I shared can also be related to how we might determine the depth at which we will be interested in knowing Jesus. Are you comfortable just to have Jesus described to you? Others can tell us all the wonderful stories they want about what Jesus has done for them, who He is and even where to find Him; but, unless we also make the effort to become acquainted with Him ourselves, we will not really know Jesus ourselves. God's Word says that you will find Him when you seek Him with all your heart and soul (Deuteronomy 4:29). Does the idea of meeting Jesus intrigue you?

Going a step further, any healthy relationship needs good communication. But, since God is a spiritual being and we are physical beings, how can our worlds meet? One way is through prayer and reaching out with your heart to the Holy Spirit to lead you into God's presence. As you will read repeatedly, God already knows all about us and He knows that unless we approach Him with spiritual eyes we will not see, hear or be able to touch Him. In His wisdom He opened our eyes and shared with us the inspired Bible or The Word of God. In a miraculous way, the Bible speaks to each one of us, breaking the barriers of generation, culture and status.

Through the Word of God we find our **B**asic **I**nstructions **B**efore **L**eaving **E**arth (BIBLE); making it a most precious and vital tool. The way for the Bible to be used effectively is if we choose to apply its truth. The way we get to meet Jesus and understand God is to spend time each day reading His Word. Remember with Jesus, you are always a welcomed friend: I will be faithful to you and make you mine, and you will finally know me as Lord (Hosea 2:20).

The Bible was written over several centuries ago by a select number of people whom God inspired to write down what He knew we needed to know about Him and how He expects us to live. These writings have been collected and placed into the book we now call the Holy Bible. It is holy because it contains the sacred words of an Almighty God to both those who are and are not His people. The Bible is the Book of Books, admirably expressing unity of the Word of God; it cannot be divided or broken down. In its contents is literature shedding great light on acceptable and unacceptable religious practices and moral behavior.

Although an exploration of the history of the Bible is fascinating and worthwhile research, our purpose in this volume is specific. Our job is to consider the Bible as a tool. What do we need revealed so that we can apply it as we work on building a stronger spiritual journey? An important start in answering that question is to know that each event recorded in the Bible signified that a new and living way was opened for all believers into the very presence of God. We find what this way is through the discipline of staying close to God daily through His Word. You may be wondering why it is so essential to read and use the tool of the Bible every day. I have made a list that I believe is helpful in addressing that question and can be used as a reference.

+ Reading the Bible tells us how to be set free from sin

+ Reading the Bible helps us recognize true and false teaching

+ Reading the Bible helps us keep the right attitude about God and others

+ Reading the Bible motivated us to be pure in thought and action

+ Reading the Bible gives us good counsel when we have problems

+ Reading the Bible gives us comfort

That all sounds really nice doesn't it? But more importantly, what's the point that's being made? In a Christian's life, happiness comes through obeying God's Word. Many people bring unhappiness upon themselves by choosing lifestyles that are destructive. I have lived that destructive lifestyle myself for several long years, caught in an eating disorder addiction, but today I am free through God's Word. Long-term happiness is cultivated by following the principles designed for long-term well being. Graciously, God has provided several positive, healthy life principles within His Word.

This chapter has mentioned many reasons to get to know Jesus through God's Word. It is so crucial that we remember who Jesus is and leave it as a legacy for our families. God wants us to pass His Word on to others, teaching them what they have been taught. Deuteronomy 32:46 tells us; Take to heart all the words I have given you today. Pass them on as a command to your children. Fear not about being equipped to teach others. God promises us that he will supply the wisdom we need to understand His Word (Hebrews 8:10); all we need to do is open our hearts to the Bible and the instruction of the Holy Spirit.

Mom's Bible – a daughter remembers:

I got an invitation to come hear my sister-in-law speak at her Community Bible Study group. They had just finished a six-week study called "God's Amazing Book." The study explored the importance of God's Word being alive in our lives and the importance of understanding how its message is intended to work.

Margie wanted to share her mother's knowledge and love of God's Word. Margie put into words how that great love mom had for the Lord and His commands impacted other lives and left an incredible legacy. Mom taught her children and grandchildren by the words in that book. Margie then showed a picture of Mom sitting at the kitchen table teaching God's Word to one of her grandchildren. It was the most precious picture of a little girl looking at her grandmother as she read to her words of life from the Bible.

After Mom passed, our family had a lot of sorting of her things to do. It is hard to go through the items of a loved one that you recently lost and who you thought the world of. One particular day, a priceless gift was found. Margie and two of her sisters came across Mom's Bible that she used in the 1990s. As Margie paged through it, she knew that she wanted it. So, she said, "In true child like fashion, in front of my two sisters, I licked it." and said, "This one is mine."

I will share with you the rest of Margie's speech and tribute to her mother in her own words and with her wonderful style:

"We know as Christians that you live here on earth for a while and then we live with Jesus for eternity. And one day we will pass from this life to the next. Mom would be here today if she could. But last February [2008], she passed away. She not only passed from this life to the next; but, she also passed the test of being a good and faithful servant of God.

After Mom passed, my many brothers and sisters and I were left with items of a life lived long and to the full. What do you do with clothes and treasures? We fought over nothing – my mom didn't have many valuables – except her Bibles. Some of us had received (or taken) Mom's Bibles from her years ago. We would say, "Mom, I like your Bible. Can I have it?" And she always gave it up.

But some of us still wanted one with Mom's handwriting in it.

I want to share a few things my mom wrote in her Bible:

+ Isaiah 53:4 – Mom wrote her name in red and she taught me that these living words were mine and now I have written my name there too.

+ Proverbs 3:13-18 – Dated 12/6/02 she underlined and noted the words, "May my children have this blessing."

+ A quote from Mother Theresa dated 2/23/91. "God didn't intend for me to be successful. He intends for me to be faithful."

+ This is my favorite. On the front page in Mom's handwriting is this:

> Betty Barrett is my name
> My family is my ministry
> Pennsylvania is my station
> Jesus is my salvation

Some people say that writing in a Bible defaces the Holy Word of God. I say it is a treasure. My nieces and nephews fight over Mom's Bible. I give you this challenge: read the words of the Bible and live your life according to what it says, and if you have three children, own three Bibles and write in every single one."

Since I was there to hear these words spoken, I can tell that there was not a dry eye in the room. Margie did a spectacular job of presenting Mom's Bible. I know that she also pleased the heart of God. I went home that day, went through all my Bibles and prepared them for my children. Do you see yet what a treasured tool a well-used Bible is? Not only are we blessed when we take God at His Word, but we also have the potential to reach countless lives. Spend a few moments and meditate on this Scripture:

Isaiah 8:16: "I will write down all these things as a testimony of what the Lord will do. I will entrust it to my disciples, who will pass it down to future generations."

Questions to Consider

+ What is *your* heart's belief; do you view the Bible as inspired by God? (Refer to 2 Timothy 3:16-17) or do you see the Bible as a book of history from long ago?

+ Is the Bible a tool you use every day? Are there things you could change to spend more time in God's Word?

+ Go back to the chapter and re-read the list that stated all the things that reading the Bible does for us. Have you experienced anything on the list? Write down what you have already experienced and what you are still working toward experiencing personally.

+ How does reading the Bible strengthen our relationship with Jesus? Have you met Jesus through God's Word? What changes in your life did you experience in those moments when you were getting acquainted with Jesus?

+ Margie gave us a challenge from her story of Mom's Bible. She shared with us that a life well lived in the instruction of the Lord is the ultimate treasure we can obtain. Psalm 19:10 tells us that the riches and sweetness of God's Word last forever…. **They are more desirable than gold… They are sweeter than honey, even honey dripping from the comb (Psalm 19:10).**

+ Now for my challenge; Read Psalm 119, a scripture about our accountability as Christians. It is a lengthy Psalm, so you may want to break it down and take a day or two to read it in its entirety. As you read this Psalm, see if you can find the answers to the following questions: What are God's expectations for His people? What must we do to enjoy life and avoid disaster? Remember, read the Bible regularly and let it hold you accountable. It is our source book and tool for right living.

The Tool of Scripture

Romans 1:19-20, Proverbs 31:30-31, Isaiah 51:7-8, John 1:1-5, Galatians 5:25

Challenge reading - Revelation 22:7-21. This will present the reason the Bible was given to us to be a mighty tool and the reason why God's promises give all believers hope to stand ready and be prepared to one day meet Jesus face to face.

What's in My Toolbox

Chapter Three:

Using the Tool of Forgiveness

Building on the Word of God – Matthew 5:23-25 –
The words of Jesus: "So if you are standing before the
altar in the Temple, offering a sacrifice to God, and
you suddenly remember that someone has something
against you, leave your sacrifice there beside the altar.
Go and be reconciled to that person. Then come and
offer your sacrifice to God. Come to terms quickly
with your enemy before it is too late…."

The Bible was written long ago and some of the
language is not the same as what we use today. The
opening verse is telling us that our relationships with each
other and God are important. They all have to be healthy;
so, if something is wrong, God wants us to stop what we
are doing and work it out. Relationships are at the heart
of who our God is. Don't waste time pretending that
something is not wrong. We sit in churches and places of
worship hurting, simply because we have not figured out
the healing potential of forgiveness.

Did you know that The Golden Rule we were taught as

children is actually Biblical? Many of us can still hear our parent's and grandparent's voices as they reminded us over and over again, "Do for others what you would like them to do for you." These words actually come from Matthew 7:12. It sounds easy. Treat people nicely and they will treat you nicely. Forgive people and they will forgive you. But for those of us who try to live by those words, it gets a little difficult sometimes, doesn't it? If you think, like I did, that forgiveness is just about apologizing, you will be surprised to be told that the act of using forgiveness as a Christian tool for reconciliation requires a lot more than that. I had a lot to learn about not only how to forgive others but also how to accept forgiveness and forgive myself. This tool is probably one of the most complicated to figure out because it deals with the heart and emotions. If you have been hurt and have feelings that you can not move past, I will pray a blessing right now that God will use the words of this chapter to loosen what is binding you; so, that forgiveness can do the work in your life that it was intended to do. If you received that prayer, then we are ready to get to the task of exploring possibly one of the most difficult tools we must have if we are to walk a fruitful path with Jesus

To use anything properly we need to understand exactly what it was intended to do. What exactly is forgiveness intended to do? From <u>The New Unger's Bible Dictionary</u> by Merrill F. Unger, 2005 updated version, we learn the following definition:

Forgiveness – One of the most widely misunderstood doctrines of Scripture.

It is not to be confused with human forgiveness that

merely remits penalty or charge. Divine forgiveness is one of the most complicated and costly undertakings, demanding complete satisfaction to meet the demands of God.

The people who have received Christ Jesus already know about God's gracious forgiveness. Therefore, it is the obligation of all believers to act upon the instructions of Ephesians 4:32, "Instead, be kind to each other, tenderhearted, forgiving one another, just as God through Jesus has forgiven you."

Forgiveness cannot be an isolated operation. It is first extended upward through God and taken outward through us. This is an integral part of the whole divine undertaking for man called *salvation*. Once God's forgiveness and reconciliation have been established in our lives, we have fulfilled one of the two greatest commandments given to us by Jesus. Jesus replied, "You must love the Lord your God with all your heart, all your soul and all your mind. This is the first and greatest commandment. A second is equally important: Love your neighbor as yourself" (Matthew 22:37-39). There are times when loving our neighbor is definitely easier said than done.

I believe that Jesus' view of loving our neighbor as ourselves is having compassion so that we can be sensitive and respect others people's needs. We should respect those around us the same way we ought to be respecting ourselves and valuing the life God gave us. Sometimes forgiveness is part of the love. God expects us to live at peace with our fellow man. Romans 12:17-19 offers advice on living at peace: Never pay back evil for evil to anyone. Do things in such a way that all people can see you are honorable. Do your part to live in peace with everyone as much as possible.

Forgiveness is our spiritual tool that enables us to deal with conflicts appropriately and make peace with others. A heart at peace that has both received and shown forgiveness paves the way for relationships, even when there is a disagreement to be resolved.

God calls us to pursue forgiveness and it involves hard work. The Bible commands us to forgive others when they have wronged us and seek forgiveness when we have wronged others. I think we can get confused while trying to base forgiveness on the merit of it being deserved or not. We tend to look at the issue instead of the command. Our DNA wants vindication and restitution for what we feel has offended us. On the other hand, pride can get in the way when we have been the offender, stopping us from making amends.

But here is the truth: forgiveness is an expression of love. We experience unlimited love in our relationship with God. That love is the resource we are to pull from that makes it possible for us to forgive others again and again. Jesus was asked often, "How many times do we forgive the same person?" In the book of Matthew 18:21-23, Peter is told by Jesus that the number of times we are to forgive someone is seventy times seven. For those interested in math, that is an amazing 490 times! This may seem impossible, but we are capable of forgiving others. Think of forgiveness as releasing your feelings about a person or situation to God, freeing others in love as God did for each of us, and in doing so He will give you His comfort and peace. Always recognize that God forgives us time and time again; I'm sure I have exceeded my 490 times for forgiveness with Him. Because of that, we can express God's love in a world that desperately needs to witness it.

Uncommon forgiveness – Joseph, governor of all Egypt:

We have a lot of good information to support the principle of forgiveness, but if it is never applied, we do not get to experience the full benefit of its purpose. Keep in mind the focus of this chapter, which is that forgiveness releases in love the guilty from the penalty they deserve. Let's see all this in action, turn in your Bibles with me to Genesis chapters 37-50. We are going to highlight the story of the journey of a young man named Joseph from his brothers' betrayal to his appointment to the second highest office in the land of Egypt. It was a journey that would span over 13 years. What began in hatred because of jealousy ended in forgiveness because of love. Read on to meet Joseph and be inspired by his total trust in God and learn from his example of what it takes to forgive. I have referenced all the chapters that this story covers so that you can read all the details at your leisure, but our discussion here will pick up on the major events of this incredible testimony. We are now headed back into God's amazing book.

Genesis 37: Joseph dreamed dreams; he was given visions by God. Joseph would tell these dreams to his 11 brothers, arousing their hatred for him. Joseph was already picked out as the favorite of their father, Jacob. Jacob adorned his favored son with an extravagant coat, causing a further division between Joseph and his brothers. Finally, the other brothers could not take any more of this special treatment and took matters into their own hands. They called a meeting and decided how to deal with the problem of their brother. They hated him so much that they wanted him gone permanently. One day, the opportunity arose; Jacob had sent Joseph out to check on his brothers. Upon his arrival, Joseph's brothers overtook him. They stripped Joseph of his coat and tossed him down an empty pit used to hold water for the flocks of animals.

At this point, what do you think you might be feeling? Joseph was only 17 years old and the people he loved the most just betrayed him and abandoned him in a dark hole. It would be a safe bet that Joseph felt totally alone and worthless. The original plan was to kill Joseph and take his coat back to their father, but the brothers had a change of heart, deciding that they could not kill their brother. Instead, he was sold into slavery for 20 pieces of silver to Ishmaelite traders who took him to Egypt.

The brothers went back to their father with the coat they had soaked in animal blood and told Jacob that his beloved son, Joseph, was killed by wild animals. Meanwhile, in Egypt, the traders sold Joseph to Potiphar, who was the captain of the palace guard.

Genesis 39-41: During his time in Potiphar's house, the Lord was with Joseph and blessed him. Joseph succeeded in everything that he was placed in charge of because the favor of the Lord was upon him. Because he was blessed, the house of Potiphar also became blessed. The household affairs were run so smoothly under Joseph's attention that he was given complete administrative responsibility over everything that Potiphar owned.

However, Joseph, who was said to be very handsome, soon caught the attention of Potiphar's wife. Day after day she would pursue him and he would turn her away. He knew that if he succumbed to her wishes it would be against God and the goodness of his master. In her anger she falsely accused Joseph of raping her and he was thrown into jail for a crime he did not commit. Once again he found the presence of the Lord was with him there too. It wasn't long before Joseph attained favor with the chief jailer. Because God was with him, everything that he took care of in the prison was soon successful.

Joseph knew that his stability was because of his deep faith in God. Because of his faith, he was able to keep his character and integrity intact. He never took his eyes off the Lord, even though his surroundings seemed to be continually changing. In jail God allowed him to interpret two dreams for other prisoners, both of which came true.

The one prisoner was restored to his position in Pharaoh's house. Joseph's only request was the man mention his name to Pharaoh. He did not. Joseph was forgotten for two more years.

It was now Pharaoh who was having dreams he could not understand. They were so disturbing that he called all magicians and wise men of Egypt to help interpret them. Everyone failed. The prisoner who Joseph helped was the chief baker. When he heard about Pharaoh's situation, he felt the guilt of not remembering Joseph. The baker quickly went and told Pharaoh all about what Joseph did for him. After hearing the report, Pharaoh sent for Joseph to be brought before him and indeed Joseph interpreted the dreams correctly because Joseph's trust was in the Lord. The details and accounts of these dreams are written out on Genesis chapter 41, but the interpretations warned that years of severe famine would plague the land. Pharaoh was so impressed with Joseph's suggestions on to how best to prepare for these events that Joseph was appointed as governor of Egypt to oversee all of its affairs. Sure enough, the events in the dreams happened just as Joseph had predicted.

Genesis 42-50: Famine was severe throughout the world. Jacob learned that there was grain available in Egypt and he sent his sons to buy some because they were on the verge of starvation. Here is where the lesson of our story all ties together. Since Joseph was then governor of Egypt and in charge of all the grain, his brothers had to go to him for the food they needed. When they arrived, Joseph recognized them instantly; but, he hid his recognition from them for a while.

As they attempted to buy their grain, the brothers encountered different kinds of troubles. Benjamin was accused of stealing Joseph's silver cup and was sentenced to remain a slave. The brothers remembered the day they sold Joseph and knew that their current troubles were the consequences of their past sins. Finally, without knowing what else to do, the brothers tell Joseph that they cannot cause their father any more pain. Going back without Benjamin, who was now the youngest of the brothers, would break Jacob's heart.

Joseph could not stand it any longer; he revealed to his brothers who he was. He was now 30 years old, and 13 years had passed since they had thrown him down that pit. You can imagine how stunned and frightened they were to think of what Joseph might do to them.

In chapter 45 verses 4-5 and 15, the miraculous tool of forgiveness is first exercised. Hear what Joseph says: "Come over here," he said. So they came closer. And he said again,

"I am Joseph, your brother whom you sold into Egypt. But don't be angry with yourselves that you did this to me, for God did it. He sent me here ahead of you to preserve your lives." Then Joseph kissed each of his brothers and wept over them and they began to talk freely with him.

After this reconciliation, Pharaoh invites Jacob to Egypt. Jacob is reunited with Joseph and the whole family, and everything that belongs to them moves to the land of Goshen, near Egypt. As the number of days for Jacob comes to an end, he blesses each of his sons. Once he is buried, the brothers worry that Joseph will now take revenge on them. In Chapter 50 verse 19-21 the second and most important act of forgiveness occurs. Joseph reassures his brothers that they have nothing to fear.

Joseph tells them, "Don't be afraid of me. Am I God, to judge and punish you? As far as I am concerned, God turned into good what you meant as an evil act. He brought me to the high position I have today so I could save the lives of many people. No, don't be afraid. Indeed, I myself will take care of you and your families." And he spoke very kindly to them, reassuring them. (Genesis 50:19-21)

Then Joseph and his brothers and their families lived happily ever after in Egypt. Joseph was 110 years old when he died. Could any of us view such a situation in such positive light? Do you see the bad things going on as possible good things that God wants to do in or through our lives?

When we decide to forgive we are making a choice. We are choosing what to forget and what we need to remember. Joseph knew it was because that God was always with him that he prospered despite how things looked. It is important that we remember where God has

Questions to Consider

+ Re-read Matthew 5:23-25. Is there business with a brother (or sister) that you have not taken care of yet? What issues are stopping you from being totally free and open to forgiveness? What do think needs to happen before you leave your comfort zone and go confront it? If this is a situation you think is impossible to deal with, pray about it for awhile first and ask for guidance from the Holy Spirit. Most of all, remember that God is always there.

+ Do you think it is possible to forgive someone 490 times? Read Matthew 18:21-35. What did you learn from the story of the unforgiving debtor?

+ From the information given in this chapter, and through the scriptures and stories we have read, how important do you think using the tool of forgiveness in our lives is? Do you see forgiveness the same way as God does or do you believe people should get what we think they "deserve"?

+ How did Joseph use the tool of forgiveness despite all the bad situations that he had encountered? Do you think he should have been angry because he seemed to be an innocent victim in each case?

+ Can you recall a situation in which you needed to apply the tool of forgiveness? Have you ever been the one who needed to receive forgiveness? What was the outcome of those situations and how did you feel afterwards? Share your story if you are comfortable; it may encourage someone to do the same.

The Tool of Scripture

1 Peter 5:7, Psalm 9:9 and 11:4-7, Deuteronomy 30:19-20, Matthew 5:43-48, John 10

Colossians 2:13-25, Proverbs 28:14, Joel 2:28-32, Romans 6: 12-13 and 19-23

What's in My Toolbox

Chapter Four:

Using the Tool of Baptism

Building on the Word of God – Galatians 3:27-29 –
And all who have been united with Christ in baptism
have been made like him. There is no longer Jew or
Gentile, slave or free, male or female. For you are
all Christians – you are one in Christ Jesus. And now
that you belong to Christ, you are the true children of
Abraham. You are his heirs, and now all the promises
God gave to him belong to you.

Before we even get into to the concept of baptism,
I choose this verse because its implication is huge. If we
go back and read in the book of Genesis, we find how
Abraham's faith established his relationship with God.
His faith was recognized and God blessed Abraham with
promises that He has fulfilled. Part of the promise was
that all children of Abraham would also be heirs to inherit
the same things. So, if we, through faith, also belong to
God and through obedience unite ourselves with Christ
through baptism, we are considered children of Abraham,
predestined to share in the same blessings from the Lord.

If you want to how what the spiritual inheritance is for those who choose to believe, I challenge you to look for them in Genesis chapters 12-25. The promise that I love and cherish is in Genesis 15:1 when the Lord says to Abraham, "Do not be afraid, Abram, [*his name before God gave him the new name of Abraham*] for I will protect you and your reward will be great."

This gives me confidence that all I need to do is believe God has me and my reward will be the daily provision and protection of an unfailing God.

Now we can define baptism and what its spiritual contribution is in our continued journey with Christ. We want to keep our relationship with Christ fresh and alive. As with any relationship, the more intimate we are with someone, the deeper it can become. When we offer tangible things that can be seen and felt by someone we love, the relationship is elevated to the next level. Through the physical witness of baptism, we make the physical statement to Jesus and everyone present that we belong to Him by choice. Our heart is melded together with His; it is an outward sign of an inward change.

Baptism is the application of water as rite of purification or initiation. This is a Christian practice. The English word *baptism* originated from the Greek word *baptismos*, which is derived from *baptizo*, meaning "to dip or immerse." There are different opinions on baptism and how the ceremony should be conducted. The focus of this discussion is not to debate or argue theology; but, to get to the heart of the significance of baptism. In baptism, the new believer enters into communion with Christ's death, burial and resurrection. In other words, it is a symbol of the regenerated soul's union with Christ. I believe, from reading what Scripture has to say, that baptism is the tool that has the greatest effect on the person engaging in it. Baptism is a life-changing act of committing all you have intentionally to Jesus. It is with that confession of faith that you are proclaiming your willingness to obey the commands of Christ. These commands are to repent, meaning to turn another way, and believe that Jesus is who God sent into the world to save it. This is not to be confused with salvation. Baptism is never the means by which we are saved or offered forgiveness for our sins. The water's only purpose is to represent a rebirth as a transformed life. The blood of Christ was poured out as the only pure and acceptable atonement, making us (the sinner) right with God. What might not be known to everyone is that baptism is an obligation. Baptism is an ordinance instituted by Christ, practiced by the apostles and submitted to by the New Testament churches.

Hear the call; obey the message – John the Baptist & the Baptism of Jesus:

The easiest way to tell you how to apply the tool of baptism is simply to hear the call and obey the message. Once we are convinced in our hearts that we want to be followers of Jesus, we should immediately obey the command to be baptized as a sealing of our decision. I thought it was much more complicated than that. My husband and I are, by the grace of God, slowly laying the foundation to begin a ministry. It is our prayer that, through outreaches such as books, speaking engagements and whatever else God leads us to do; we can spread the love of Jesus. We go to a church that practices baptism by full immersion. It was unfamiliar to us to see several people a week walk into a pool in front of about 1,200 watching eyes and get dunked for Jesus. Wanting to understand this, we searched the Bible for an answer. Both of us were baptized as babies. Our teaching was that you only needed one baptism. So, of course, that is what we did with our children, too. But through our research, and prayer, we were convinced of three things. First, you need to make your own confession, repent of your sins and accept the forgiveness of Jesus. Second, baptism is a command of obedience, as we have been studying. Third, although the baptism of Jesus was different, He was obedient to the call and was baptized before starting His public ministry. And if Jesus did not begin His ministry until He was totally obedient to His father, who are we to do any less? Our goal as Christians is to have our lives match that of Jesus. I can tell you that my husband, Tom, and I both felt deeply the call to go and be baptized. We were baptized together with our families as witnesses. A few months after our baptism, our younger daughter felt the same call and she was also baptized. When Christ serves as a model, the impact in our lives goes on and on.

Let's visit another baptism. It started again with a message and followed by obedience. The story takes place in Matthew 3:3-17 and 4:1. John the Baptist was aggressive and passionate about his mission. He was the one foretold to come before the Messiah and prepare the way (Luke 1:8-17). His days were spent in the Judean wilderness warning the people to repent of their sinful ways and return to the Lord. John also preached the message that he was not the one they were waiting for; one much greater than he was coming. John's was a baptism of repentance and he baptized anyone who confessed and repented. Those who obeyed the message to "make ready the way of the Lord" and believed "the Kingdom of heaven is near," were symbolically immersed and purified in the Jordan River.

One day, Jesus was baptized by John. His baptism was unique both in its significance and purpose. Jesus did not make confession; He had no reason to repent. At first, John did not want to baptize Jesus because he knew who He was. He did not feel worthy even to tie the laces on His sandals. Jesus assured him that it must be done, because He must do everything that is right. It was an act of ceremonial righteousness, which was appropriate before beginning His public ministry. Jesus' threefold office included that of Prophet, Priest, and King. As priest, the Levitical law (Numbers 4:3) required that all priests be consecrated at about age 30 (which Jesus was). In His baptism in the Jordan, this consecration to Jesus' redemptive priesthood comes into the clearest view. By "doing everything that is right," our Lord meant fulfilling the righteousness of obedience to the Mosaic Law. This was the ceremonial and moral law given through Moses. Jesus' baptism fulfilled this law as follows: first, He was washed by water. Second, He was anointed. When John "washed Jesus, the heavens were opened and the Holy Spirit came upon Him like a dove." This was a divine anointing appointing Jesus as eternal Priest and God's approval for Him to begin the work of redemption. If you have also been following along in the Bible, verse 17 says, "And a voice from heaven said, 'This is my beloved Son, and I am fully pleased with Him.'" Right after His baptism occurred Jesus was led into the wilderness to be tested by the devil and to prepare for His ministry. The good news is that He was led by the Holy

Spirit, assuring Him that God was with Him every step
of the way.

The last point about baptism is that we don't have to
wait. Don't be fooled into thinking that you need to wait
until you're good enough, cleaned up enough, or together
enough before you step into the water. To be honest, we
are not perfect, or we would not need God. We can try
and maybe get a few things right, but God loves us already.
He just wants us to listen to Him and connect ourselves
to Him. Listen to the Apostle Peter's explanation of
using the tool of baptism. Consider the words carefully.
May they speak as an encouragement to you to always do
immediately what the Lord puts in your heart to do.

Acts 2:38-41(emphasis added): Peter replied, "Each
of you must turn from your sins and turn to God, and be
baptized in the name of Jesus Christ for the forgiveness of
your sins. Then you will receive the gift of the Holy Spirit.
This promise is to you and your children, and even to the
Gentiles, all who have been called by the Lord our God."
Then Peter continued preaching for a long time, strongly
urging his listeners, "Save yourselves from this generation
that has gone astray!" *Those who believed* what Peter said
were baptized and added to the church – about three
thousand in all. They joined with the other believers and
devoted themselves to the apostles' teaching and fellowship,
sharing in the Lord's Supper and in prayer. This is not one
isolated account of this kind. Stories like this go on and
on all throughout the Bible, where we see people believing
and getting baptized in the name of Jesus. Is it your time to
add your name to the list of believers who took advantage
of the tool of baptism? In closing, it also says in Acts 8:12
that Philip, who was a deacon and servant of the Lord,

was sharing his message of the Good News concerning the Kingdom of God and the name of Jesus. As a result of what he shared, many men and women were baptized.

I pray that, if you have not already heard a message that convinced you about Jesus, that God would open your heart so that you hear the truth. Jesus Christ was revealed as God's Son by His baptism in water and by the shedding of His blood on the cross – not by water only, but by water and blood. So we have three witnesses – the Spirit, the water and the blood – and all three agree. And God has testified about His Son (1 John 5:6-9).

Questions to Consider

+ How would you define baptism? Do you think all believers need to be baptized? Why or why not? (Read Romans 6:3-6 & Acts 19:4-5) Have you been given any new insight on your view of baptism?

+ Does salvation or baptism come first? What is the difference between salvation and baptism and is the order we perform them important? Acts 10: 44 & 47-48 says; Even as Peter was saying these things, the Holy Spirit fell upon all who had heard the message.... Then Peter asked, "Can anyone object to their being baptized, now that they have received the Holy Spirit just as we did? So he gave orders for them to be baptized in the name of Jesus Christ. (Take note that the process always starts with hearing, then believing, and then action.)

+ Is baptism offered to anyone? What do we find out in Acts 10:45?

+ How is the baptism of Jesus different from any other? Refer back in the chapter to the information shared. Or re-read Matthew 3. Consider especially verse 15.

+ If baptism has been established as a command of Christ, is it a believer's obligation to fulfill what has been instituted? Are Christ's commands negotiable? Read 1 John 2:3-6 and write your answer based on those verses. Is what you read different from what you might have thought?

The Tool of Scripture

1 Corinthians 1:18, Titus 3:3-8, Psalm 26:6-8, Colossians 2:9-15

Leviticus 8:4-9 (this is part of the ordination of the Priests), Isaiah 61:10-11

1 John 2:15-17, 2 Corinthians 6:1-2, John 3:5-8 & 3:22-28, Acts 8:30-40

What's in My Toolbox

Chapter Five:

Using the Tool of a Community of Believers

Building on the Word of God – Romans 15:5-7& 13 –
May God, who gives this patience and encouragement,
help you live in complete harmony with each other –
each with the attitude of Christ Jesus toward the other.
Then all of you can join together with one voice, giving
praise and glory to God, the Father of our Lord Jesus.
So accept each other just as Christ has accepted you;
then God will be glorified…. So I pray that God, who
gives you hope, will keep you happy and full of peace
as you believe in Him. May you overflow with hope
through the power of the Holy Spirit.

Some tools you will only need once. Salvation and
baptism are two examples. We may, from time to time, in
our hearts re-commit ourselves to Christ (my prayer is
that it is daily habit); but, the act is done once and forever.
But most tools we will keep in our Christian toolbox are
meant to be used over and over again. Ideally, our lives are

always changing as we grow in our faith journey, so we need to be prepared to adapt by pulling out old tools to be used in a new way. This is the case as we reach out and experience the church as God had intended. What was God's vision for His church? I believe God's vision is for us to be unified in Christ and be involved as part of each other's lives. I will go so far as to say that God planned to have most of worship done outside of church. Pretty bold, huh? It was never the intention that we "play" church on Sundays, hear a message that makes us feel good about ourselves and then be dismissed for the week, forgetting anything spiritual for the next six days. God wants His believers to meet together.

In Acts 2:44-47, we see God's people living out what a community of believers belonging to Christ should look like: all the believers met together constantly and shared everything they had. They sold their possessions and shared the proceeds with those in need. They worshiped together at the Temple each day, met in homes for the Lord's Supper, and shared their meals with great joy and generosity – all the while praising God and enjoying the goodwill of all the people. And each day the Lord added to their group those who were being saved.

Does that sound like church as you know it? Are you spending time getting to know the people you worship with? Are you talking about the Kingdom of Heaven in your home and joining the fellowship in the homes of others? That is all part of church. Living in community with other Christians brings about positive change in our behavior as we strive to show that we are true ministers of God. 2 Corinthians 5:17 speaks of the change we experience as we step out into the world for Jesus. It tells us that those who become Christians become new persons. They are not the same anymore, for the old life is gone. A new life has begun!

Being committed to Christ means we are required to get involved with all people. Learning to devote our hearts, minds and bodies is central to a life of faith. Jesus never said that we had to do it alone. That is why He called His disciples to come together as a community of believers, strengthened by the Holy Spirit to edify and encourage each other as they help give the lost the hope of Christ. If we are the called people of God, then we need to live using the tool of connecting with each other and the community to shine the love of Jesus to a world overshadowed by darkness. Listen to the words of Jesus from the gospel of Matthew 4:19-20 (emphasis added): Jesus *called out to them*, "Come, be my disciples, and I will show you how to fish for people!" And they left their nets at once and went with Him.

I can promise you that we do not learn how to fish for people by leaving our pews on Sunday and staying involved with only what is affecting us. If you are one whose habit it is to hear the message of the gospel and not share it, then you have missed the message entirely. Church is not just there to make us feel good; that is only part of it. It is there so that we can be unleashed to share its message with the world. There are six more days during which we are to be reading God's word, applying the message, coming together for prayer, and reaching out to the needs of others. That is done outside of church with many small groups of like-minded and committed hearts meeting together with a passion to see the Good News spread and more people's lives to be reconstructed from pain to victory.

Like the human body, the church, which is the body of Christ, was created to look like Him and was put together with many different parts to make it function well. The Apostle Paul teaches us this concept of being one body with many parts. In Paul's first letter to the Corinthian church he writes that the human body has many parts; but, the many parts make up one body. So it is with the body of Christ. We have all been baptized into Christ's body by one Spirit, but God made our bodies with many parts and He has put each part where He wants it. In fact, some of the parts that seem weakest and least important are really most necessary. So, God has put the body together in such a way that extra honor and care are given to those parts that have less dignity. This makes for harmony among the members; so, that all the members care for each other equally. Now all of you together are Christ's body and each one of you is a separate and necessary part of it (1 Corinthians 12:12-27).

Are you beginning to understand how vital a healthy functioning community of believers is and the impact it could make on our society? The term *believer* is used a lot. Its meaning is to remain steadfast, to be persuaded of God's revealed truth and to adhere to and rely on God's promises. Once we believe that, our lives as Christians are to bear fruit and be devoted as witnesses to that which we believe in (Galatians 5:22-23). The fruit grown in our lives is dependant upon our faith. Faith contains three features that all believers need to have:

1. Saving Faith – inward confidence in God's promises and provisions in Christ for the salvation of sinners.
2. Sanctifying Faith – daily living upon the benefits of Christ for sustaining our faith. Once

we have experienced saving faith, we are "in Christ" and we use His power to participate in living a saintly life.

3. Serving Faith – acting upon the truth of our divinely bestowed spiritual gifts. This faith is used according to a person's individual leading by the Holy Spirit as to where the divine enablement and appointment of these gifts will be for service.

A person who has been converted, or convinced, has exercised saving faith in the work of Jesus. Therefore, in becoming a believer, a person has joined the ranks of a community of believers who hold an esteemed position of continuing in Christ's atoning work. Jesus confirms this charge in the gospel of John 14:12, "The truth is, anyone who believes in me will do the same works I have done, and even greater works, because I am going to be with the Father."

It has been stated that a community of believers has the responsibility of doing the work Christ started which is showing all people that He is the only way to the Father (John 14:6-7). But there is another side to what coming together as the body of God's people is for. Before we are able to persuade others about God, our spiritual relationship must be in good condition. We need ways to practice a closer walk with God and keep our character traits looking as much as possible like Jesus'. The more we place ourselves in the presence of God in all we are and all we do, the more we are building the foundation of a godly life. This is where the second part of a community of believers comes in. We already read earlier how the early church interacted and took care of each other. They were following the example showed to them by Jesus. No one who is a Christian is on the journey alone. Jesus was not isolated; therefore, neither should we. He walked with people, talked with people, ate with people, taught people, studied with people, prayed with people, challenged people and held people accountable for their actions, behavior and decisions. Jesus established Himself as a part of community in every way. That is how the church needs to see itself too.

How do I connect to a community of believers and what does it mean for me?

Most of the information shared so far about how to use the tool of a community of believers has focused on making sure that the message of the salvation of Jesus gets out because, we ourselves, have believed it first. Now we need to take the next step and make it personal. Having an effective Christian life is living upward (how we see God), inward (how we relate to God) and outward (how we express God).

Taking care of our relationship with God is of high priority. We know that our daily readings of God's Word, prayer and attendance of Sunday worship services are key practices to focus our minds and heart on God. However, solidarity can only take us so far. If we stand alone to make sure we are in the right places and doing the right things in life, we only have ourselves to trust. You may find this hard to believe (as I often do), but we don't always have the right answers or make the right choices. See if these verses do not prove what has been stated: Proverbs 16:1-3 – We can gather our thoughts, but the Lord gives the right answer. People may be pure in their own eyes, but the Lord examines their motives. Commit your work to the Lord and then your plans will succeed. Proverbs 12:15 – Fools think they need no advice, but the wise listen to others. Proverbs 20:18 – Plans succeed through good counsel; don't go to war without the advice of others.

These Scriptures tell us that we need accountability in our lives and that is why we need to connect ourselves with a community of believers. Most people are not fans of having to explain themselves to others. They perceive accountability as invasion of privacy and accuse people of just wanting something to gossip about. People also equate accountability with restrictions and opening up dark parts of our lives that we would rather keep hidden. It's not always comfortable, but it is necessary. Whatever your personal opinion of accountability is, when we know we need to answer for our behavior and lifestyle, you can bet that we will do all we can to make sure we are measuring up to what others expect. Accountability means answering to someone who sometimes may ask tough questions. But there is some good news; accountability is not an idea that allows some random person to invade your life and tell you what they think about it. We are to choose the person who holds us accountable. This person is called an accountability partner and this is probably one of the most important ways we connect ourselves to the community of believers. As Christians, we need the strong support and Godly council of the members of Christ. In order to go about looking for an accountability partner, follow these simple steps: Step one, include God and ask for His guidance as you seek a partner. Step two, for not so obvious reasons; your partner should be of the same sex. Third, this person should possess the qualities listed in these verses: Exodus

18:21-24 – But find some capable, honest men (women) who fear God and hate bribes. They will help you carry the load, making the task easier for you.

Do you see now what having accountability means? If we are unaccountable, we are free to go where our desires lead. This can be a destructive and dangerous game. It is crucial to hear the truth that God is the One holding us all accountable, whether we accept it or not. He sees all, knows all; nothing is hidden from His sight. One day we will have to give an account of the things we have done and failed to do. Ecclesiastes 11:9 makes this caution: Young man, it's wonderful to be young! Enjoy every minute of it. Do everything you want to do; take it all in. But remember that you must give an account to God for everything you do.

The message is clearly to enjoy life; but, to stay within God's guidelines. That is what we gain by using the tool of the community of believers who help make us aware of maintaining harmony between our earthly and spiritual lives. There is so much in the world today that can deceive us; it is a long list, you can be sure of that. Being involved with people who meet regularly outside of the church building is our greatest defense in living a life for the Lord. Having "church" in our homes provides ways to be aware of what strongholds and temptations are against us. Face it; the things that have our attention are what we will go after. Paul gives the church strong reasons why we, as believers, need to band together in a world that wants darkness to rule over light. The Apostle Paul was not one to sugar coat what he knew for certain that the Lord led him to preach. Most of his messages have an urgent call to take a look at your life, your values and your convictions and to rid yourself of anything that is in conflict with God. How would you like Paul as an accountability partner? Not many of us would get by very easily I'm afraid. Let's go back to his letter written to the church of Corinth as he explains why we are to be bonded together with our brothers and sisters in Christ.

2 Corinthians 6:14-18 & 7:1 (paraphrased): Don't team up with those who are unbelievers. How can goodness be a partner with wickedness? And what union can there be between God's temple and idols? We are the temple of the living God. As God said, "I will live in them and walk among them. I will be their God, and they will be my people" Because we have these promises, dear friends, let us cleanse ourselves from anything that can defile our body or spirit. Let us work towards complete purity because we fear the Lord.

The point here is for us not to be in a spiritual bubble, excluding those who do not yet know the Lord. Rather, we should be like full sponges. I heard this illustration on Christian radio and I thought it was great. Before a sponge is used it is empty and flat; but, as a sponge is used, you can see the difference in its size and feel the difference in its weight. The sponge becomes full of water and when you squeeze it in your hands the water runs out of it from every pore. The water completely filled every inch of available space the sponge had. That is how our Christian life should be. We should be so full of the Holy Spirit that it just flows out of us and into others. Every area of our lives should be completely saturated with Jesus. The love that fills us up for the Lord needs to be squeezed out into the life of another person.

Being part of a community of believers is such a great tool for us. This is the core group of people who we can count on to encourage us on our walk with God as we study and talk about the Scriptures together. Proverbs 27:17 says that people learn from one another, just as iron sharpens iron. Having such a group in our lives allows us to enjoy a unique bond with people who will come to our aide when we need help, pray for us when we need guidance, and uplift us during hardships. It means that we care for them and they care for us as Christ cared for the church (John 13:34-35).

The best way to become part of a community is to link into it. Look for Bible study groups, adult discussion classes or prayer groups. Or you can be bold and invite people into your home for Christian fellowship. You might be surprised to find out that you are the sponge someone has been waiting for! If you agree with the following words, you are qualified to impact your community: anyone who loves a pure heart and gracious speech is the King's friend (Proverbs 22:11).

Remember the words Jesus left us: there are still greater things to be done here. "And so it is, that many who are first now will be last then; and those who are last now will be first then" (Matthew 20:16). A community of believers moved by the Spirit of God can radically turn the world's thinking upside down.

Questions to Consider

+ Do you perform worship outside of church? Are you connected with a community of believers in any way Monday-Saturday, such as Bible study, prayer group or a community group in someone's home?

+ Is meeting outside the church building important? Read Hebrews 10:25, Matthew 18:20, 1 John 1:3- Luke 2:46, Acts 2:46 What are some of the things from those Scriptures that the community of believers comes together outside of church to do?

+ Is there a personal story that has made an impression on your life because you were involved with the community of believers? Can a new believer contribute just as much as a long-time believer to the body of Christ and the community?

+ Can a Christian produce the fruit of the Holy Spirit in his or her life and not be part of a community of believers? (Refer back to Galatians 5:22-23) Why or why not? (Refer back to Acts 2:42)

+ Did Paul's letter to the church of Corinth challenge the way you spend your time and who you spend it with? (2 Corinthians 6:14-18 & 7:1) Are there greater things you could be doing for the Kingdom of heaven? Remember the words of Jesus from John 14:12.

- Challenge: Spend time in prayer and ask God to speak to your heart specifically about where you fit into the community of believers. Be prepared to hear Him.

The Tool of Scripture

2 Corinthians 5:18-20, Titus 2:6-8, 1 Samuel 14:1-15,
Proverbs 23:17-19 & 24:1

Psalm 16:2-4, Luke 24:35-49, Romans 15:14, Ephesians
4:11-16, 3 John 5-8

What's in My Toolbox

Chapter Six:

Using the Tool of Faith

Building on the Word of God – Hebrews 6:10-12 – For God is not unfair. He will not forget how hard you have worked for Him and how you have shown your love for Him. Our great desire is that you will keep right on loving others as long as life lasts in order to make certain that what you hope for will come true. Then you will not become spiritually dull and indifferent. Instead, you will follow the example of those who are going to inherit God's promises because of their faith and patience.

We do not want to overlook the tool of faith. Faith is like the heartbeat keeping our relationship with God alive. When we trust God with the biggest things we are hoping for and believing that He will fulfill them, that is faith. It is like saying, "Okay God, I can't do this, but I know you can. I believe in my heart that because your promises are true, You are there." Faith is not about what you are asking God for; faith believes in who you are asking. Jesus said, "The truth is, you can go directly to the Father and ask

Him, and He will grant your request because you use my name… and you will receive" (John 16:23-24). It is not a surprise that so many people believe that God has let them down in some way. We are so worried about our situations or too busy trying to fix things ourselves that we forgot to go to God and ask. God blesses us even when we don't ask or don't deserve it, because He is good. But, imagine what would happen if we had faith enough to ask God into our lives and rule over every situation? What if we included Him in everything that is going on with us? It is sad that we perceive ourselves to be so intelligent that we think we know more than God does. Here is another sad fact: less than ten percent of Christians ask God's opinion on major decisions. That tells me two things. One, there is a lot of disappointed and hurt people out there. Two, people do not have the patience to allow faith to work. We have to wait on God (Psalm 37:7). There are so many reasons why we should wait on the Lord. One reason I will share is that He knows best what we need and when we need it. Another part of faith is accepting what God's plan is rather than being convinced ours is better.

What is faith? It is the confident assurance that what we hope for is going to happen. It is the evidence of things we cannot yet see (Hebrews 11:1). That is one Bible verse that I have committed to memory. It has helped me remember, countless times, how to use the tool of faith. I can be confident, hopeful and patient that God is doing something in my life, even though I may not always know what it is; but, I do know that if I have faith I will see it. We trust what we put our confidence in. If we place our confidence in God, we already know some of the great things He has done. Therefore, I know that I can have faith that He will take care of me, too. I think we can agree that we all have faith in something, but not many of us can distinguish if we can be certain of that which we have trusted. If we count on ourselves and our own abilities to get us through life, there is the risk of someone else coming along and doing things better than we do. If we count on our money to get us where we want to be, it could easily run out. If we count on somebody else to be responsible for our happiness, they will let us down; it is a big job to satisfy another person's needs all the time. If we count on our charm and good looks, well let's face it, time takes its toll. Beauty is fleeting, as Proverbs 31:30 says, "Charm is deceptive, and beauty does not last, but a woman who fears the Lord will be greatly praised."

It may seem a bleak picture to imagine life if we place our faith in something other than God. Only if we trust in Him will all those things that we are hoping for and more are added on to us. Matthew 6:33 tells us that He will give you all you need from day to day if you live for Him and make the Kingdom of God your primary concern. How do we put that information to use? How do we, in faith, live for God and make His Kingdom our concern? Well, in a word, we are saying, "yes" to what God wants. Faith in God reveals that we are willing to trust God with our very lives. This means that we are willing to follow His guidelines for living as outlined for us in the Bible because we have been convinced that this is best for us.

Is our faith that deep? Are you or I willing to let God carry us through life? Picture a tight rope walker hundreds of feet in the air with no net below. We can believe that he will make it across, but it is not until we let him take us across on his shoulders, totally relying on him for our safety, that we demonstrate faith that he can do it. What allows us to cross the rope with someone else carrying us is faith in the ability of that person. One thing we can have confidence in is that our God has never once fallen! He is still seated on His throne, high and exalted (Isaiah 6:1-4). Now, that's the type of track record that I can put my faith in. Faith is a tool; it is the tool God gave us to use that brings us hope that we have a strong and trustworthy anchor for our souls. If we use our faith by being confident in the promises that God has given (and there are many), we get God's attention. How do we do this? How would one even go about getting the attention of the Maker of the Universe? We do this by building a foundation of faith with two unchanging principles. Number one, the beginning point of faith believes in God's character – He is who He says He is. Number two, our faith will not be strong unless we keep our eyes on Jesus, on whom our faith depends from start to finish (Hebrews 12:2)

Without believing those two things, it is impossible for us to please God. Faith is what assures our salvation and wins the approval of God. "For in just a little while, the Coming One will come and not delay. And a righteous person will live by faith. But I will have no pleasure in anyone who turns away" (Hebrews 10:37-38).

In Hebrews chapter 11 we are given a list of great examples of faith. I have been referring to this book of the Bible a lot, as we have been taking a looking at faith and how it pertains to our Christian toolbox. I suggest that you read this portion of Hebrews. I believe it gives the richest insight and explanation on how to use faith in our lives and how we are blessed as we exercise our faith. God's Word is always the authority, so it is good for us to make a habit of returning to it. As you spend time in your Bible, challenge yourself to discover whether you are a new or seasoned believer as you read those stories that this passage in Hebrews covers. Read on and you will encounter even more stories confirming that God is in control. Incredible situations were overcome and battles were won because of the tool of unshakable faith. If you want your faith to become strong or mature, God must be at the center of it all. A victorious outcome does not happen any other way. 1 Peter 1:7 tells us, if your faith remains strong after being tried by fiery trials, it will bring you much praise and glory and honor on the day when Jesus Christ is revealed to the whole world. What an encouragement to you and me! Through that promise we are no longer victims of our situations but have the opportunity to experience God. If we allow God to redeem us in our suffering, our faith is deepened as we move closer in the process of becoming people who are holier and stronger as time goes on.

The persecution, suffering and trials that take place all around us are life-changing events. As did the people in Biblical times, we have a choice to make. Do we retreat, letting go of faith or do we move steadily forward in faith? No matter what the outcome, because we know in whom we have trusted, we gain victory when we walk in faith. What events are going on with you? Are there any mountains you are facing, any rivers you need to cross or any storms that need to be calmed? Have you picked up the tool of faith yet?

A Giant, A Boy, and A Rock – A king in the making: (Referenced in 1 Samuel 17:1-58)

In this corner of the ring we have the Philistine champion Goliath; a trained and skilled warrior. This tower of a man stands over nine feet tall, wearing body armor weighing over 125 pounds and an arsenal of weaponry, including a bronze javelin and a heavy thick spear. In front of him he carries a huge shield. Goliath's mission: defeat the Israelite army.

On the opposing side, representing the Israelite army stands his opponent, David. This young, teenaged boy has no military training and the extent of his pedigree is that he is the son of a shepherd. His weapons of choice – a rock, a staff and a leather sling. David's mission: rid the people of Israel of this giant and its enemies.

Does this appear to be a fair fight? Humanly speaking, and at first glance, probably not. But what is yet to been seen is that God, through David's faith, was certainly up to something. Let's take a ring-side seat and find out. The confrontation is about to begin.

Goliath comes out swinging. Every day he would shout across to the Israelite army taunting them to send someone brave enough to fight him. He further mocks them by saying that he alone would fight the whole army. Everyone in the Israelite army was terrified and as soon as they saw Goliath they would run away.

Entering into the ring now is David. One day he showed up with supplies and food for his brothers who were on the front line of the battle field. The men shared with David what was going on, telling all about the fear throughout the army that Goliath was causing. David could not believe what he was hearing. He started asking questions around the camp, "Who is the pagan Philistine anyway, that he is allowed to defy the armies of the living God?" (Verse 26). Even though he was ridiculed by his older brothers, the youth continued to investigate this huge opposition. Word of his interest got back to King Saul and David was summed to report to the king.

David began to use his faith in his mighty God. With confidence he told the king that he planned to go and fight the enemy. King Saul's reaction was what we would expect. "Don't be ridiculous! There is no way you can go against the Philistine. You are only a boy and he has been in the army since he was a boy!"(Verse 33). But that did not deter David; he was persistent. He refused to be defeated by doubt. Remembering what the Lord had already done for him, he placed his total belief and trust in Him. David told the king that there was no reason to fear, because God has always been his protection and will not stop now (Verses 34-35).

The debate with King Saul quickly ended with David firmly declaring, "The Lord who saved me from the claws of the lion and the bear will save me from this Philistine!" (Verse 37).

Saul finally consented, "All right, go ahead," he said. "And may the Lord be with you" (Verse 37).

Going to the battle field, prepared to get into the ring is David; he is armed with the finest armor that King Saul could provide. However, as the heavy gear was being strapped on, there was a problem. The youth was not used to all the weight and constriction it caused. He took everything off and began to arm himself with the things he trusted. Most of us would not feel very secure about picking up five smooth rocks, a shepherd's staff and a sling as our weapons for combat, but that is exactly what David did. His foe, Goliath, felt the same way about the meager amount of artillery that was about to be used against him. The thought that he could be taken down with a stick and a few stones insulted him to the point of exasperated anger. He shouted out words of outrage to the young opposition and promises of a most gruesome end to our hero. To all of this, David replied with his own idea of what the outcome of this match was going to be.

Here is where faith is used as a tool and the reason why, through that faith, we can face any giant in our lives in full assurance of victory. Take notes – this is so good that I will let little David tell you himself in a big way! Be cautioned; since we are experiencing David's battle with Goliath, it does get a little graphic in the details.

David shouted in reply, "You come to me with sword, spear and javelin, but I come to you in the name of the Lord Almighty – the God of the armies of Israel, whom you have defiled. Today the Lord will conqueror you, and I will kill you and cut off your head. And then I will give the dead body of your men to the birds and wild animals, and the whole world will know that there is a God in Israel! And everyone will know that the Lord does not need weapons to rescue His people. It is His battle, not ours. The Lord will give you to us!"(Verses 45-49).

With that, David reached into his shepherd's bag, took out a stone, and hurled it at the Philistine giant. The stone hit its mark, sinking into the forehead of Goliath. The mountain of a man that looked impassable stumbled and fell to the ground, taken down by the rock of faith. David had delivered a knock-out punch and a most unexpected result. Since David had no sword on him, he ran over and took his enemy's sword and proceeded to do all that he said he would do (Verses 48-51). After that, the rest of the Israelite army ran to finish the fight, overtaking and plundering the Philistine camp.

This was most certainly a life-changing event and a defining moment for a young teenage boy who faced his giant dressed only in the armor of faith in the Lord. Because of his faith, God blessed David's life in many ways from that day on; it was the beginning of all the great things he was to do. He not only married Saul's daughter but also became a mighty warrior for the army of God's people. And not to give away the whole story of the Bible, but this boy was the very same man who would one day be named King David, a man after God's heart, all because he stepped onto the battlefield in faith that God would secure the victory. I pray that we all just show up, face our giant and ask God to overtake it, and believe that He will. First we believe, then we trust, and now we have faith.

Questions to Consider

+ Where is your faith? Are you seeing only giants in your life? Are you willing to walk toward them, prepared to face your battles in faith with God? Refer back in the chapter to the story of David and Goliath or re-read 1 Samuel 17. How does this story help us to have bold confidence in our faith?

+ If everyone trusts in something, what are the things you trust in? Can you think of a time when what you trusted in failed? What was it? Can God ever fail us when our trust is in Him? Why? Read Hebrews 6:16-18.

+ When has using the tool of faith been the biggest resource to you? What is the only way that we can receive the faith we need? Read Romans 10:17.

+ Did you know that a way to increase our faith is to forget the things we should forget by letting go of past disappointments or trails and seeking to remember the things we should, such as each time that we have seen God's work in our lives? Joseph was a man who knew exactly what this meant. He was able to have faith in God during all his trials because he knew what to forget and remembered the things he should. Read Genesis 41:50-52 – What did Joseph choose to forget? What did Joseph want to remember? How was it possible?

+ Read Psalm 3. List why we can trust using the tool of faith and all the things that our God delivers. Remember: *The Lord is a shelter for the oppressed, a refuge in times of trouble. Psalm 9:9.* If God moves your heart, consider writing your own statement of faith and committing it to the Lord.

The Tool of Scripture

Jeremiah 29:13-14, Luke 8:4-8, Romans 12:2-3, Revelation 2:7&9-10, Galatians 5:5

Job 42:1-6, Joshua 14:10, Colossians 2:6-10, Amos 9:5-6, Isaiah 30:18-19, James 5:15

What's in My Toolbox

Chapter Seven:

Using the Tool of Serving

Building on the Word of God – Romans 6:12-13 – Do not let sin control the way you live; do not give in to its lustful desires. Do not let any part of your body become a tool of wickedness to be used for sinning. Instead, give yourselves completely to God since you have been given new life. And use your whole body as a tool to what is right for the glory of God.

A popular measure for success in one's personal life is the ability to afford to pay people to do things for you. People are hired to mow lawns, wash cars, clean houses, cook, etc. – in other words, they who think they are successful, have servants. This way of thinking gets turned on its head by the life and teachings of Jesus. Jesus taught that the highest goal in life is not having people serve us but by being the one who serves others. The whole idea of service cuts across the grain of what we see in the world. We are taught to watch out for Number One – help yourself first. One of my favorite ideas that epitomize narcissism is that only the strong survive. In this world lacking in desire of true service to one another, the weak are the ones who are seen as those who should be serving the strong. But the inner strength and quiet humility it takes to perform acts of service for our fellow humans is the test of a successful character. Character is the one thing that has no price by which you can buy it; you have to earn it yourself. Could it be that this is the precise reason Jesus places so much emphases on serving? Perhaps, just maybe, Jesus is suggesting that we take a look around us and move out of our small world of "self" and into the big world of considering others. The way to use the tool of serving is to remember in your heart and mind that serving is others-centered rather than self-centered. Serving God and others is the essence of an effective Christian life. It is the only way we get to experience the joy of impacting another life, because we invest time, energy and work into it. Serving is, therefore, the opposite of selfishness.

I can't blame anyone for wanting to know what they are buying into. That's smart. Never sign anything before you read the fine print. Jesus feels the same way, which is why He will always be our example of anything He asks us to do. The question that some may have is what it means to be a servant. This devotional has already laid some of that foundation by presenting the concept that you must move away from your own wants and needs to meet someone else's. The next thing we will venture into is the way Jesus showed us how to be a servant. In the most striking picture of servant hood, Jesus humbled Himself in obedience to the Father, leaving His heavenly throne and coming into the world to serve it.

Philippians 2:3-8 reads, "Don't be selfish; don't live to make a good impression on others. Be humble, thinking of others as better than yourself. Don't think only about your own affairs, but be interested in others, too, and what they are doing. Your attitude should be the same that Christ Jesus had. Though He was God, He did not demand and cling to His rights as God. He made Himself nothing; He took the humble position of a slave [the meaning of this word is the same as *servant*] and appeared in human form. And in human form He obediently humbled Himself even further by dying a criminal's death on a cross."

Jesus showed us that serving others is leaving our position and status to join the reality of someone else's very different way of life. By performing the tasks of a servant, He models for us how far we are to go in serving each other. Attempting to be selfless and reaching out to where people are hurting has definitely placed us on the right path, but that is only half of what using the tool of serving requires. If we want to use this tool to our full Christian capacity, we must align the attitude of our hearts to go with our actions. My conviction of this is based in what we learned in Philippians 2:5 – your attitude should be the same that Christ Jesus had. As we acquaint ourselves more and more with the servant attitude of Christ, we know a few of the words best describing it are *humble, compassionate, loving, merciful* and *full of grace.*

Throughout His three years of ministry on earth, Jesus devoted His life to serving both God and people. Jesus bent down and washed the feet of His disciples so that they in turn would know how to do the same for others (John 13:1-17). He revolutionized our understanding of leadership by demonstrating that being a servant comes from the top and moves downward. Read Matthew 20:24-28; the disciples receive the only key to turn on the tool of serving – understanding the order of priorities. Pay close attention to verse 28. Jesus makes one of the boldest statements about who He is and where He has placed Himself. "For even I, the Son of Man, came here not to be served but to serve others, and to give my life as a ransom for many" (Verse 28). If Jesus declares Himself to be a servant, who are we as Christians not to do so as well? What a challenge to all of us, especially to those seeking a spiritual relationship with God. Jesus is up front about the cost.

Missionaries past – Amy Carmichael's story

When I was praying to find the right story to illustrate the concept of using the tool of serving as Christ served, I was lead to some great people in history. Praise the Lord for modern technology; I searched online for famous names of missionaries and found many wonderful stories via the internet. For example, Amy Carmichael, born in Northern Ireland in 1867, was the oldest of seven children. Her father's death when she was 18 profoundly affected her. This event caused Amy to think seriously about her future and God's plan for her life. Before she even conceived the thought to become a missionary, God blessed her with a glimpse of what it means to have a heart for other people. On one nasty, windy winter's day, she and her family were walking home from church when they spotted a poor old woman in rags wrestling with her meager bags. Amy recalls how she and her siblings all felt the urge to offer assistance to the woman. But to her sadness, they did not. The youths were embarrassed to help because they did not know how the other respectable people walking with them would react to helping someone obviously viewed as beneath them.

As they walked on, they passed a beautiful Victorian fountain where Amy claims to have heard an audible voice recite the words from 1 Corinthians 3:12-14 (take time to read this passage). When Amy turned to find who had said this, she saw no one but people moving about the streets. Before this time, Amy admitted to being preoccupied with her social life, but at this moment she felt God calling her to settle some things with Him.

In September 1886, the Carmichael family traveled to Glasgow, England, to attend a conference. The purpose of this conference was to promote awareness for attaining a "higher Christian life." At that conference the hand of God was felt in Amy's life. She realized that nothing could be more important than giving all she was and all she had to live her life for Jesus, who had done the very same for her.

In 1895, the Church of England Zenana Missionary Society commissioned her to go to Dohnavur, India. Amy served there as God's devoted servant for 56 years, never once returning to Ireland during that time. The image of the old woman struggling with her heavy bags remained in her memory and inspired her to love what the world had deemed as unlovable. That overflow of love resulted in the establishment of the Dohnavur Fellowship in India, which became a place of safety for children. This refuge saved more than a thousand children from neglect and abuse.

To her credit, Amy was a prolific writer, with 35 books published. Writing had been a talent for her since childhood. An unfortunate accident in 1931 kept Carmichael confined to the Dohnavur Fellowship compound, but that did not keep her from living out what the Lord gave her to do. She continued on in obedience, total commitment and selflessness devoted to her beloved Lord and Savior.

God may or may not station you in some distant land, as He did Amy Carmichael; however, you can be sure He has a plan for you to use the tool of service. We can be sure by reading the Gospel message that He wants us to bring the light of His eternal hope and forgiveness to the world, especially the part we are in. Our attitude regarding being Christ's torch should not be "Why me," but "Why not me?" If our desire is to be of service in God's kingdom, our response when called on can only be that of the Prophet Isaiah:

"Then I heard the Lord asking, 'Whom should I send as a messenger to my people? Who will go for us?' And I said, "Lord, I'll go! Send me" (Isaiah 6:8).

We have to be ready to go where the Lord sends us at all times. We just shared a wonderful story of a woman who said "I'll go." It didn't matter to her that she was taken far away from her life and placed in a remote country for many years. But what if we are called to be close to home and for a short season? I think that God still wants us to approach it with the mindset of doing everything for Him.

Missionaries present – Montana's story; Ready to pay the cost:

Another young girl answered the central question that God wants anyone who claims to have a relationship with Him to settle in their heart. How can I serve God in my life today? A servant is loyal and obedient to his master, even when it's not convenient. The story of Montana illustrates just such an attitude. Montana is a young girl who is 12 years old, and her mission field is her middle school. Each day she tries to brighten the halls by being a better example of living than what she sees around her. Montana possesses a self-assured confidence of who she is and knows that she is very much loved by God. She is not shy to share her faith or show people compassion; she always seems to be the underdog's advocate. In her prayers at dinner, she often lifts up those students she knows who had a rough day or possibly dealing with hard situations in their lives. Her heart is tender toward what others feel. This philosophy is unique to the style of our modern-day schools and often puts her in unpopular places with some of her peers. They can't seem to figure out why some build up what others only want to tear down.

I don't want to give you a picture of a little Mother Theresa in blue jeans. This pre-teen is my daughter, and trust me, she has her rough days, like we all do. But how she is handling the pressure of her first year of middle school has made an impression on my husband and me. Montana loves softball. Ever since fifth grade she has been talking about being on the school softball team when she was old enough.

Early in this first middle school year, with much hard work, effort and good attitude, Montana made the basketball team. She enjoyed playing the sport; so, she continued to improve throughout the season. The personalities of her teammates seemed the opposite of hers. They gave her a lot of trouble with hurtful remarks and excluded her from the "in crowd." With each practice and game Montana continued to show up, give her all and cheer her team on. She ended the season feeling good about what she accomplished and the fact that she stayed true to who she is.

Softball season is now right around the corner and I have been waiting for this for a long time. I too, loved the sport of softball and played many seasons through my school years. I was excited that my daughter was getting the chance she had been waiting for. One day recently, Montana came running into the house from the bus stop with great news about the team: she was going to be the manager! "What?" I said to her.

I asked her how this could be. She had been waiting for years to play on the team and she has real talent. Her eyes filled up with tears, and she ran up the steps. I could not understand what made her do this. As I went after her to have a talk, my husband reminded me that Montana deals with people differently and that I need to keep that in mind

I really wanted to understand her thinking about all this, so I asked her to open up and explain it to me so that I could support her, because I was struggling as I watched my daughter step aside from something she had wanted to do for so long. During our conversation, she shared how the girls who are on the softball team were the same girls who had been on the basketball team. Although it was not making her totally happy, the decision was made. She did not want to take their ridicule on the field as she had on the court, but Montana felt there was something she could still offer. It was placed on her heart to serve the team. Her heart is telling her that by being manager she could be a part of the team and get to know the girls better. This is an excellent example of serving others even when it is not easy.

I share this story because it is so refreshing to see someone so young have a passion to live her life true to serving God and others (Matthew 16:25). Montana decided to take a situation that is uncomfortable and, instead of feeling bad, she is making it work for the benefit of herself and others. In the eternal picture, she is getting the biggest reward, because anyone who serves with a loving heart and goes willingly wherever it is that God sends them will one day hear God say to them, "Well done, my good and faithful servant. You have been faithful in handling this small amount, so now I will give you many more responsibilities. Let's celebrate together" (Matthew 25:23).

Don't those words just rush right to your heart, filling it with encouragement? Using the tool of serving and displaying the image of God to the hurting, hungry, lost or confused in the world is never a waste of our time. Whatever we do here on earth for someone else, no matter how big or how small, we are doing it as unto the Lord also (Matthew 25:31-46). I am excited for such a privilege. Are we bold enough to pray and ask the Lord to send us out for Him, even if we don't know where we are going?

Questions to Consider

- Make a list of three things: what you have done to use the tool of serving, how you are currently using the tool of serving, and what you hope or plan to do to use the tool of serving. Look over your list; does it give you any insight that you find helpful?

- Have you been personally touched by someone else's act of selfless service? What were similar elements within the two stories we read about Amy Carmichael and Montana? What was different about the situations and type of service that Amy Carmichael and Montana were called to? Could you pick up and move to a faraway land if God asked you? That question is for personal reflection; it is a deep question that requires thought and prayer. Spend time journaling your thoughts.

- A lot of Bible verses were referenced throughout the chapter. Take time to go back and look them up; note the verses that were particularly meaningful to you and why or any Scripture that might have convicted you of something that God wanted you to hear.

- The Scripture of Matthew 25:14-30 tells the Story of Three Servants. As you read this story pay attention to these points:

1. Just like the master giving the three servants money, God has given each of us the resources of time, ability, and opportunity.
2. Like the servants, we choose if we are going to bury or invest those resources and put our gifts to use to earn an eternal return.
3. It doesn't matter if we have much or little; the Master expects us to invest ourselves wisely and boldly into His service.
4. Do you know what resources you have been entrusted with? How might you get the maximum return on those resources with regard to the Kingdom? What if you were to invest your gifts in spiritual profit instead of placing them in secular values?

Luke 6:38: If you give, you will receive. Your gift will return to you in full measure, pressed down, shaken together to make room for more and running over. Whatever measure you use in giving – large or small – it will be used to measure what is given back to you. This is a promise from God. What does it mean to you?

The Tool of Scripture

Galatians 6:4-5, Jude 21-23, Revelation 22:12-13, Joshua 24-14-15, John 4:34-38

1 Samuel 2:1-10, Proverbs 11:25, Ephesians 3:8-9, 2 Thessalonians 3:6-15, Acts 19:10

What's in My Toolbox

Chapter Eight:

Using the Tool of Your Witness

Building on the Word of God: Acts 1:8 – "But when the Holy Spirit has come upon you, you will receive power and tell people about me everywhere – in Jerusalem, throughout Judea, in Samaria, and to the ends of the earth."

The words from Acts chapter one describes the job Jesus left us to do. As He ascended into heaven to be with the Father, He spoke the words quoted in verse eight to His apostles. They were no longer able to see the One who came to save them. All that was left was what Jesus had begun to do and teach and the people who could testify about what they saw. This was the charge He left to all those who remain – *on all occasions, talk about the Kingdom of God, to people everywhere.* Can we handle it? Are you ready to tell the world what you know about Jesus? Will we continue the work that He came here on earth to do? The power to live a dynamic Christian life hinges on our willingness to tell others about God's love. It is through the stories we personally have that allow the world to learn how Jesus touches lives. How do you know Jesus? I am certain that you know of His love because someone told you who He is.

We modern-day saints have the same commission that all those who followed Jesus before us had – to be His representatives. Don't fear the opposition, because we are not defenseless. Jesus told His followers, including us, that the power of the Holy Spirit will come to empower them to speak and live for Christ. Think of the Holy Spirit's power as fuel and energy being poured into us, enabling our lives to work for the Lord. It is also because of the power the Holy Spirit brings that our witness can be used as a mighty tool for God's kingdom. But if we rely on our own energy to fuel our Christian walk, it is not going to be enough. Our stories are not about what we accomplished, but what the Holy Spirit has done to open our eyes and hearts to Jesus.

As we continue filling our Christian toolbox with valuable recourses, we will become more and more productive with the changes we are making in our lives. If we exercise the things Jesus teaches us to use, hopefully others will be inspired to try a new way of living too. Using the tool of our witness is one of the more effective ways we can help someone else's life also become radically altered, because if we can show people evidence of Jesus living in us, they will want to experience the same thing. Staying plugged into the ultimate power source, God's Holy Spirit, we can shine brightly as we tell the story we know about Jesus.

The word *witness* may conjure up ideas of awkward religious laws. We may doubt if we are worthy enough to talk about Jesus to others or even feel we have not done all the right things to make us a good example of His name. It is ironic that the one thing that does make us worthy of sharing the love of Christ is what we are most afraid of – not being perfect. Religion will often cause us to develop a way of faulty thinking that is the opposite of what God really wants to tell us. How many of us hold this thought: "Isn't witnessing a job for trained people, like pastors, priests and missionaries?" In truth, witnessing is simply telling someone what you have experienced. Just turn to John 9:1-34 and read the account of Jesus healing the blind man. After he was granted his sight, he could explain only an account of what happened to him. He said to the crowd of people, "I know this: I was blind, and now I can see!" He used the tool of his witness to shout to everyone what Jesus did for him.

According to the Bible, every follower of Christ has the privilege and obligation of bearing witness of Jesus. Christians should always be ready to tell the story of how they became acquainted with Jesus and what that experience was like. That story, unlike any other, is a promise that if we acknowledge God on earth, He will acknowledge us in heaven (Luke 12:8).

Using the tool of witness takes all kind of appearances. Yes, we do sometimes see people on the street corner screaming messages of hell and damnation into a bullhorn. I don't think we need to discuss how that style of spreading God's love might not be for everyone. Fear may cause a few of us sinners to repent, but God is more interested in gaining our discipleship for the long haul. God is not a bully; He doesn't want us to believe in Him just because we are scared of the alterative. When people do things out of fear, it never lasts; soon the heart grows weary and they give up. People need encouragement when we share God's Word with them, not fear of condemnation. Psalm 119:28 reads, "Encourage me by your word." That is why the message of John 3:16-17 needs to be declared even louder. That should be our approach in how we use the tool of our witness, simply by bringing the encouragement of Christ to a non-believing world.

Our witness needs to declare that lost people matter to God and that it is not His will that any perish or be snatched from His hand. This is one part of the story we all should have in common, is it not? Weren't we all at one time lost until we were found by a loving God? Titus 3:4-5: "But then God our Savior showed us His kindness and love. He saved us, not because of the good things we did, but because of His mercy. He washed away our sins."

I think that the concept of communicating what God has done in our lives to others is what the tool of witnessing is made for. Witnessing, like anything else that does not come naturally to us, may take some time to get comfortable doing. Don't be too hard on yourself in your attempts. Read John 7:12-13, and you will see that even those closest to Jesus and knew Him the best struggled to speak up sometimes. Remember, a true testimony to God's Word is our actions. If we are not living His word, chances are that people are not going to believe it. 1 Peter 2:12, "they will see your honorable behavior, and they will believe."

If the tool of witnessing is kept in our toolbox and never taken out, it can't be of any use to anyone. We each have a unique style representing God's love to the world. All we need to do to use the tool of our witness is devote ourselves to Jesus and be willing to share our story. Let God handle the rest of the details. God will show us how to tell others about Him as He brings those people into our lives who He wants us to talk to. Our part is to introduce them to Jesus, plant the seed and trust God to bring the harvest (Luke 8:4-15).

Natalie's Story: Something Beautiful

As we listen to people's story, we find that we have more in common than we think. I was with my older daughter, Jessica, at our church's annual girls' youth group retreat weekend. I was excited for the two of us to spend time together. Jessica is our middle child and I thought that a weekend of one-on-one time with her would be perfect. We attended the Revolve All-Access event for teen girls. This is a weekend geared toward using all different creative venues to get to the relevant issues girls struggle with most. The performers addressed topics such as body image; self-esteem; relationships with family, friends, guys and faith in God. The weekend was packed with people using the tool of their witness.

One of the people who shared her story with us was Christian artist Natalie Grant. Natalie revealed her heart as she told thousands of girls and women about how Jesus healed the pain no else could see. She made herself vulnerable, describing her heart-wrenching struggle with bulimia. This caught the attention of my daughter and me right away. The story Natalie told was very similar to mine. At that time, our family was in the healing stages of my own eating disorder. I had struggled with anorexia and the devastation caused by anorexia is similar to that caused by bulimia. I know that Jessica has vivid memories of the pain my sickness caused. That special weekend seemed to be a gift in the restoration process of our relationship, because we learned that there is no such thing as perfect people, just people who need to be forgiven. Through God's love we can even be free to forgive ourselves, which was the hardest part for me. 1 Peter 5:10-12 says, the God of all grace after you have suffered for a while will strengthen, perfect, and settle you.

Natalie's passion in urging people to pursue Christ was evident as she progressed through her story. She shared how she does not want her appearance, career or people's opinion to be the things that define her. In her first book, <u>The Real Me: Being the Girl God Sees</u>, Natalie relates in detail her experience with her eating disorder, her struggle with self-image and the flaws she fights. The story is a testimony of God's healing power in a broken life. Her songs tell us that the most attractive aspects about a person are on the inside and are related to the deeper things in life, like family. Relationships and faith in Christ are more valuable than what others think.

Natalie's witness affected me deeply, not because she is famous and an incredible singer, but because it encouraged me and reassured me that I was not alone as I continued to move forward in my journey. She taught me that it is okay to be who God created me to be and when He looks at me, He doesn't see my flaws, He sees something beautiful. That has been the purpose of my mission in giving the same witness that Natalie does to women, especially my two daughters. My point is that I believed her because I had experienced what she had and she showed me Jesus in the message from her mess. Our story may not reach everyone, and that's all right, but we can be sure that it will touch someone.

On Natalie Grant's website I found a statement she posted in her blog which sums up her story and includes everything about how to use the tool of our witness to give glory to God for His hand in our life. In these words; she says, "Listen, I'm not a hero, I'm just human. I wasted so many years worrying about things that don't matter and striving for things that are just not important. I admit that I have been way too self-involved and self-absorbed most days to even take notice of the rest of the world. But thank God He woke me from my selfish slumber and stirred me to action. I only have one life. I want to make it matter."

We may not all be able to have a stage as our platform, but we do have the world if we take the time to go out into it. Our stories are all different, and I am sure that someone somewhere is waiting to hear yours!

Questions to Consider

+ Back in the chapter we were asked the question, "Can we handle it?" The "it" refers to telling others about Jesus. Before the tool of our witness can be used, we need to know what our story is. Take some time to write your story out. Who is Jesus to you? What has He done for you? Include all the details you can remember about the time when you first believed Jesus. Then, ask yourself the question again, Can *you* handle telling that story to someone else?

+ Why do you think God wants us to tell the world who Jesus is through our witness? Why would people believe what we have to say about Jesus? Read Acts 9:1-31, Saul's conversion. Take note of who he was before he met Jesus and after he met Jesus. Write out anything you learn through Saul's encounter with Jesus and then answer the questions with this Scripture in mind.

+ Read Jesus' prayer in John 17:13-25. Who is He praying for? What is He praying that they will do? How are they supposed to do what Jesus is asking? What else is revealed to you though this prayer about using the tool of our witness?

+ Based on all the Scripture readings we have looked at, if you are a Christian, do you think that using your tool as a witness for Jesus is a privilege and responsibility that God has given to those who are

His? Do you think it is possible not to share our story if we have truly met Jesus?

+ Here is a question for prayer and reflection. Are there any individuals with whom you want to share your story but have not? If in fact it is something you have experienced yourself, what is holding you back from telling them about Jesus and God's love? Write down their names. Look at each name and ask God to guide you in these relationships and to help you know the best way to introduce them to the Jesus you know.

The Tool of Scripture

Esther 4:13-17, Psalm 138:8 & Psalm 139:3, 1 Corinthians 14:1, 1Kings 8:56

Daniel 12:3, John 14:1-2, Ephesians 1:3-5, 1 Thessalonians 2:4-8, Jonah 3:1-10

What's in My Toolbox

Chapter Nine:

Using the Tool of Tithes and Offerings

Building on the Word of God – Malachi 3:10 – Bring
all the tithes into the storehouse so there will be enough
food in my Temple. If you do, I will open the windows
of heaven for you. I will pour out a blessing so great
you won't have enough room to take it in! Try it! Let
me prove it to you!

God is asking us to test Him. If we faithfully use the
tool of our tithes and offerings, the windows of heaven will
be opened and blessings rained down. But the promise
depends on us. God says, if we will, then He will.

More intriguing than what we will receive is why God
would want to prove what He says to us. I believe it is
because the concept of tithes and offerings originated in
the heart of a giving God. Think about it; God pours on
us more blessings than we can possibly conceive. He has
already given us the gift of life, the gift of love and the
gift of salvation. The most awesome blessing of all is that
all of God's gifts to us are priceless. They are unique and
beyond compare with human giving, but they also cannot

be received unless we take and open them. And now, God is asking that we bring all we are to Him.

Tithes and offerings broken down to their simplest form are forms of giving. When we give of our money, time, or talents, we are to bring them to the Lord with a sincere heart. On the surface, giving appears to be sharing possessions, wealth and income with those less fortunate, but it must all be shared willfully. The result of investment of our time, energy and talent is represented by the tangible possessions we accumulate. But our character – who we are – is represented by what we have invested of ourselves with God and others. The Bible promises that the more we give, the more we receive (Mark 10:17-27). This does not necessarily refer to material wealth, but we are assured that we will become rich spiritually and gain eternal rewards. God does indeed promise bountiful blessings for those who give generously and choose to follow Him, but we should never give just to acquire something in return. That motive violates the role of giving as an act of love. A Christian's motive for giving needs to be because God commanded it and our hearts believe it. The way we actively use the tool of tithes and offerings is to give what we materially have and offer everything we are for heaven's Kingdom.

A tithe is the first ten percent of our income and money, set aside. It is to be given to God as an offering of thanksgiving for what He has provided for us. While much of the Old Testament talks specifically about giving one tenth of what we make to God, the New Testament encourages us that tithing is about giving what we can sacrificially and with a grateful heart rather than literally. For many, this may mean giving far more than ten percent.

We must each make up our mind regarding how much we should give. The amount we give is not as important as the eagerness we have to give. One must never give reluctantly or in response to pressure. Instead, let your attitude be filled with the knowledge that the more we give of ourselves, the more God's generosity flows out of us. God wants us to give out of what we have, not what we don't have. He only asks that we give out of the gifts that have been given to us so that we can honor Him with the best we have to offer. Proverbs 3:9-10 says, "Honor the Lord with the best part of everything your land produces. Then He will fill your barns with grain." Basically, what we are told here is that God will provide enough for all that we need and plenty left over to share with others if we place Him first in our lives.

Tithing is also a form of discipline. Voluntary use of this tool makes us aware that the things we have are not as important as trusting that God is at work in our lives, no matter what the situation may be. How many times do we struggle with this thought, "I'm just barely making ends meet, how can I afford to tithe?" It is tempting to hold back from giving God what is His when we think there is not enough left for us. We are faced with a choice. Will we deny God's greatness and authority in our lives when the relationship calls for sacrifice, or will we remain committed and obedient to what God requires? If we offer our tithes when we think we can't, we are putting our love for and trust in God into action and not just words. If we always consider our material needs and wants first, we will never think that we have enough to give. The secret to being happy is residing in God's constant care and being content with what we have. Whether it is much or little, we can live abundantly if we sacrifice all we have and rely on God for the rest. Philippians 4:18-19 tells us, "Our sacrifices are sweet smelling, acceptable to God, and pleasing to Him. And the same God who takes care of me will supply your needs from His glorious riches, which have been given to us in Christ Jesus." This passage from Scripture confirms that if we are faithful in giving, God is faithful in supplying.

As long as we can accept that our tithes and offerings are to come out of the depths of a pure heart for giving, then we understand how to use this tool as we add it to the toolbox of our Christian lifestyle. It is not complicated, but as we said, it requires commitment.

This checklist will keep our mind focused on the reasons why it is good to be a cheerful giver.

<u>Why should we give?</u>
God commands it (Exodus 22:29 & Exodus 23:19)
It demonstrates that God is first in our life (1 Chronicles 29:6-14)
It reminds us that our possessions are not the most important things we have
(Matthew 6:25-34)
It allows us to witness that God provides (1 Corinthians 2:9)
It teaches us to have a grateful heart and to live content in the Lord (Romans 8:28)
God is glorified (2 Corinthians 9:10-11)

Allow this list to be your guide as you offer your tithes and offer your talents to the Lord and you can be sure that God is pleased with all that you are giving. As the Scriptures say, "The person who wishes to boast should boast only of what the Lord has done" (1 Corinthians 1:31).

A lesson from wrong advice: Giving even when it hurts

I can remember a message given one Sunday on tithes and offerings. This lesson was given during our yearly stewardship campaign, which seeks to get everybody pumped up about reaching into their wallets and keeping up with or possibly increasing their giving pledges. I completely agree that we need to be reminded regularly about all the reasons that our commitment to giving is important and foundational to us as Christians. The guest pastor who was preaching that day covered the topic in the usual manner we come to expect when the church talks about money and how we need to view our possessions as belonging to God. He went over the need to invest our money, time, talents, and whatever resources we have and offer them as gifts to be used for heavenly service here on earth. The church survives on the giving of its people.

Then the pastor did something unusual; he shared a personal story of confession. He told us that he cannot speak on giving without being reminded of the time he counseled someone to rob God. An elderly woman had come to him with her electric bill. She was desperately trying to keep her head above water and pay all of her bills. She came to ask the pastor a question, "Does God want my offering or for me to have electricity?" In her mind, there was no way she could do both. The pastor tried to put her at ease and told her to pay the bill. Relieved, she left and did as she was told, but the conversation lay heavy on the heart of the pastor. He knew he was wrong. He told someone that had looked to him for advice to put God second, intentionally telling her that her problem was too big for God to cover. God was never given the chance or asked to meet her need. Sometimes obedience means taking a risk that we may have to go without light, but God is in control and may have a lesson for us to learn. If we are not left in the dark, how do we know how bright the light can be when we no longer take it for granted that it is always going to be there? Listen to what James 1:2-3 offers us in encouragement: "…whenever trouble comes your way, let it be an opportunity for joy. For when your faith is tested, your endurance has a chance to grow."

You might question how someone could rob God when He doesn't need anything that we have, but we can. The Scripture Pastor used to illustrate his story to us was Malachi 3: 8-9, which clearly speaks of God's displeasure when we hold back what we are expected to give. "Should people cheat God? Yet you have cheated me! But you ask, 'What do you mean? When did we ever cheat you?' You have cheated me of tithes and offerings due to me. You are under a curse, for your whole nation has been cheating me."

This may not seem earth shattering; you may think that the woman was paying her bills and the pastor didn't want to see her suffer. No real harm was done in this little story. But there was; whenever we are disobedient to what God says, we hurt our relationship with Him. This point was the main point of the story – the church didn't suffer from not having the woman's money, but the real shame was that her eyes were taken off of the Creator and placed on the created.

The one benefit from the decision related in the story is that the pastor who shared his mistake with us showed us that we all mess up and our humanness is why we need God in our lives. He also went to the woman and gave her much different advice the second time. We can always trust the Lord and see if He doesn't do exactly what He says!

Questions to Consider

+ Take a personal inventory. What type of giver are you? Are you a cheerful giver? Is it important that God is honored first with your money, time and talents?

+ Read Matthew 6:1-4. Jesus teaches about giving to the needy. Does this passage point anything out that you may need to do or do differently? How does Jesus say we are to give our gifts? There are two rewards that are mentioned. What are they? Which one is the one we should be seeking?

+ What do tithes and offering mean to you? Write your definition. How do you use this Christian tool in your life? Is tithing a priority to you? How do you honor God with your gifts and talents?

+ Read Luke 12:22-34: Jesus teaches about money and possessions. What is the message that you get from this passage? Where should we be looking for our real treasure and what should we be working for? What do the things we store up on earth reveal about our heart?

+ Could you give up everything you own for the Lord? Is Jesus welcome to all that is yours? Read Matthew 16:23-24 and Luke 9:21-27, the cost of following Jesus.

The Tool of Scripture

Deuteronomy 28:7-8 & 11, 1 John 3:17, Mark 10:17-27,
Psalm 49:6-20, Isaiah 58:7

1 Corinthians 16:2, Romans 8:17, Philemon 1:6-7,
Proverbs 17-20, John 6:1-15

What's in My Toolbox

Chapter Ten:

Using the Tool of Fasting

Building on the Word of God – Joel 2:12 – The Lord says, "Turn to me now, while there is time! Give me your hearts. Come with fasting, weeping and mourning."

The tool of fasting is another tool that can only be used as a one-on-one benefit in our relationship with God. This principle of fasting applies to our walk with God. As we remain spiritually filled with God's presence, the more we will consciously walk away from evil things, namely Satan. Spending time fasting and empting ourselves of bad habits and temptations enables us to move closer and hear from God. Fasting is not a time to test God to see what we can get from Him; but, it is a time to obediently listen and follow His will. An authentic fast is one that is lead by the Holy Spirit. This can only be done by spending less time in the world and more time in the word of God. The tool of fasting helps us guard against the pitfall of complacency and self-sufficiency. Those two things place God aside in our lives. The same question is asked over and over again when we replace God with self-reliance, "If we have all we need, why do we need God?" That seems to be the mood in our sophisticated day and age, but it is also nothing new.

Every act that takes us away from God has the undesirable consequence of separating us from Him. As we learn how to properly use the tool of fasting, we start the process of pondering our own actions (or lack of action) in our relationship with the Lord. Essentially, we are turning our heart over to Him to be opened and examined. "Give me your hearts," the Lord urges (Joel 2:12). God's plea is the same today as in the days of the Prophet Joel, as are the consequences of what we choose to do with our lives. Fasting is the method we use to answer God's call to bring Him our hearts and everything that is inside so we can deal with it together.

Knowledge should always come before application. The background, intention, meaning and concept of fasting need to be explained, so that, this tool can be correctly used and benefit us the most. We want our lives to be built up by each Christian tool available. Fasting is a way to manifest a still profounder humbling of the soul before God. The Hebrews, in the earlier period of their history, practiced fasting whenever they found themselves in trying circumstances, misfortune or bereavement. This was their custom of giving God their undivided attention so that He would again look upon them with favor. But this practice goes back further than that to the early ages of man, when people used fasting as a way to handle their superstitious and religious beliefs. Because of the belief in many gods, great emphasis was placed upon what the earth produced and what could be hunted. Sources for food were uncertain, so fasting was often compulsory, as superstitious ignorance tied this compulsion into an expression of divine will. Fasting became a religious duty. As a result, we find that fasting as a religious duty is almost universal.

The idea of fasting has two definitions. First, in Hebrew the word means to cover the mouth. Second, in Greek the word means to abstain. Both meanings imply the sacrifice of personal will, which is the idea that gives fasting all of its value. The word *fasting* is not found in the Pentateuch, which is composed of the first five books of law given to Moses. The expression used in the books of law to describe the act of fasting is "humble your souls."

As we follow the history of the Christian Church into the New Testament, we delve into the life of Jesus. In the gospel of Matthew chapter 6 verses 16-18, Jesus sternly rebukes the Pharisees for their hypocritical display in the type of fasts they observed. Jesus never appointed any fast as a part of His own religion. His practice of putting this tool to work in His life was through voluntarily fasting so that His mind would be unencumbered with earthly matters in order to devote himself solely to the contemplation of divine things. The custom of Jesus was to combine prayer and fasting as a way to stay close with His Father, so that, He could walk in obedience to Him. The combination of prayer and fasting helps establish our commitment as Christians. We need to understand the distinction that Jesus makes between fasting and "hungering and thirsting" for the Lord. The absence of food is not the goal of fasting (Matthew 9:14-17). Achieving a deeper hunger for the things of God and a thirst for the living water Jesus provides is what we are to crave (John 4:1-15).

The method of fasting, duration of fasting and conditions of the fast all are personal. This tool will have the most significance in our life, and if we come away stronger in the Lord, it will affect others around us as well, because we will be changed. Using the tool of fasting is most effective when it is done under the guidance of the Holy Spirit. Along with all the specific details we listed of what your fast will include, there are other issues that need to be settled before you begin. The most important is that you have cleared your mind, removed as many distractions as possible, and opened your heart to receive whatever it is God will reveal to you. If you are not expecting to hear from God, then the rule of thumb is that you are not prepared for a fast yet, and that is okay. We need to be honest and embrace our relationship with the Lord where it is. As long as our goal is to see it grow, we are right where God wants us.

Fasting must be done as scripturally as possible and it must be done with unbroken prayer. I can promise you that anything we do for the Lord will be confronted by Satan; when we are weak, he will try to remove our eyes from God. When Jesus spent His time of prayer and fasting in the dessert for 40 days, Satan showed up to cause trouble whenever he could. Read the account in Luke 4:1-13 and take guidance from Jesus' example. Knowing God's Word was the tool that Jesus used to drive the devil away. I won't ruin the surprise because I know you will want to pick it out yourself. The protection of the Lord is our strength. Dress yourself fully in God's armor each day (Ephesians 6:10-18) so that you can resist the attacks that are sure to come.

Finally, if you have never used the tool of fasting before, I suggest that you seek wise council from those who have. Listen to their experience, heed their advice, and ask them for their support and prayers if you decide to go forward. On our Christian journey, we all need others who will come along with us and share the walk.

My personal experience with the few times I have used the tool of fasting to hear God speak into my life is that it works. I can testify of what I know; I did get the answers I was seeking, but I will also admit that I am still sharpening this tool and learning all the advantages of using it. The church I belong to recommends this practice. When there is real work that the church wants to accomplish globally or locally, our pastor will challenge us to consider joining him in prayer and fasting to ask God's favor and guidance in whatever it is we are looking to do. He believes that big things are only going to happen with the help of God. The time of fasting is always obligatory, and the church body is always encouraged to share anything that God has revealed.

I want to place the last tool we will talk about in our toolbox the same way we started – in God's Word. There are a few references explaining the intention and result of fasting as a Christian tool in the Book of Joel. The intention of fasting is paying attention to God and expecting to hear a word from Him. Joel 2:13 gives these instructions you may find helpful:

… "Don't tear your clothing in grief; instead, tear your hearts." Return to the Lord your God, for He is gracious and merciful. This is telling us that something going on in our hearts moves us to action.

The result we should desire to gain by fasting is also given in the book of Joel 2:27-29: … Then you will know that I am here among my people of Israel and that I alone am the Lord your God. "Then after I have poured out my rains again, I will pour out my Spirit upon all people. Your sons and daughters will prophesy. Your old men will dream dreams. Your young men will see visions. In those days, I will pour out my Spirit even on servants, men and women alike." This is telling us that we want something between God and us to happen as an outcome of our fasting. Fasting is being so closely connected to the Spirit of God that once it is over we see the things He is saying to us and recognize His supreme presence in our lives. Sometimes the way God decides to show Himself to us is miraculous and mysterious.

We are essentially making a promise to God when we enter into a time of fasting. That promise is that we will give our full attention to the spiritual and place food, drink and things that we hunger in of the flesh out of our reach. Proverbs 20:25 reads, "It is dangerous to make a rash promise to God before counting the cost." As Jesus warned the Pharisees, so also must we be warned before we embark on this endeavor. Are we performing our acts of righteousness to look good in front of man or are we with sincere heart approaching the throne of a King we want to continue to please?

Finally, our concern above all else with fasting must be our motives. When our motives are right, our actions most likely will be right too. But wrong motives give birth to unwholesome actions. Our motives stay guarded when we act in wisdom, intentionally striving to meet God's standards. Jesus said, in Luke 6:45, that our actions expose our value system. What we do shows what we really believe. God wants us to achieve fullest potential. Do your actions clearly show that you are living by the values taught in the

Bible? A wise person reminded me that fasting without prayer is simply starvation.

"What I learned not to do" – A lesson from Mrs. Kempf:

The theme of the Mother in Love Series has been based on the Scripture verse Titus 2:1. When we model excellent Christian behavior, to the best of our ability, others notice and will learn how to follow Jesus closer because of what they see. I have been blessed with having many such examples of women with deep faith and love for the Lord in my life. These women of wisdom are the glue which binds the spiritual lessons together that must be handed down to those who are young and growing in the ways of God. Well seasoned words will bring forth a well spring of knowledge. With that in mind, I was not surprised to find myself back at the door of Mrs. Kempf who has all the characteristics of a Titus 2 woman. My request was that I wanted her to tell me a story about how she used the tool of fasting.

I, up to this point, have had minimal experience with fasting beyond head knowledge. Mrs. Kempf once again welcomed me to her kitchen table where we sat down and talked. The conversation started off with her saying, "What I can tell you through my times of fasting is what God showed me not to do." It was important that Mrs. Kempf made me aware that we do not try to fast to save the world because that job already belongs to Jesus. Not every prayer request or issue is a call to a fast. What we can do to is pray that people get saved or healed; but their salvation is between the person and God. Fasting is used as a time to hear and obey God when He calls us to do it.

Her "hero" fasts, as she called them, never bore much fruit. It was trial and error like anything else we try to learn until we find out what works. Through obedience (which is the major element in our relationship with God) and prayer God revealed to Mrs. Kempf what He wanted her fasts to look like. The biggest lesson she learned is that we must never do things for God looking for something back; we do it out of the sacrifice of love. God untimely blesses us because He is good, not because of what we think are good deeds.

I am paraphrasing; but, Mrs. Kempf told me that what changed her habits of fasting is a conversation she had with a person whom she respected. He said, "Catherine, do you really think that because you are not eating a certain food God will save someone? They get saved when they get saved by the grace of God." She said that was enough to convince her to rethink her approach. We will be most successful in using the tool of fasting when we prepare for it. Our intention must be commitment to purifying our hearts before God and resisting temptations that would distract us from that. By determining ahead of time how we will respond to the situation of focusing only on the spiritual world and ignoring our flesh God gets more of our undivided attention.

Mrs. Kempf told me that she once prepared a weekend like that for herself. Her plans were set to go on a group retreat; but, the flu kept her at home unable to attend the trip. What she decided to do was still make this a time set apart to be with God. Mrs. Kempf already was not eating much because of her illness, so she did other things to ensure her full focus was on spending time with God. She unplugged her phone, turned her television off and spent the time that she was awake in Scripture reading and recording in a notebook everything the Lord was saying. And do you know what? Mrs. Kempf was shocked to find out that she missed nothing at all because the Lord gave her all the same Scripture that the people who had gone on the retreat received. The point is that when our hearts are open and God is invited, He will come in. It doesn't matter what we remove from our life to make room for God. It can be food, dessert, spending idol time on the computer or reading magazines rather then the Bible; what matters is making Jesus Christ the center of why we are doing it.

It was also important to Mrs. Kempf that she reinforced to me that God knows our inner most body structure and our chemical make up. Some of us may have health issues, such as Mrs. Kempf who is a diabetic, which restricts the body from being deprived of food for extended periods of time. She gave examples of how fasting is still a tool that everyone can use. The book of Daniel gives a good blueprint to follow for those who desire to experience a Spirit filled fast and maintain their health. The reading in Daniel 1:8-16 gives us wonderful encouragement that we do not have to compromise our health while we are in a time of fasting.

Having the spiritual guidance of Mrs. Kempf in my life is a gift. Each occasion I have had to spend one on one time with her has enriched my understanding of God's Word and my walk with Him. As we ended our time together that day, she shared a personal discipline with me that she does everyday, and has for years. God commands His people to observe a time of physical and spiritual refreshment. That is why we rest on the Sabbath and sleep at night. It was explained to her a long time ago by a nun that resting is a type of fast, because when you are sleeping, you are not eating and you are obeying the command of God to rest. The other part is when you wake up in the morning and before you eat or do anything; you pray a word of thanks for the day and God's protection for it then open the Bible. The passage of Scripture you turn too first is your Word from God for the day. Whatever word you are given is to be written down and thought about all day as it comes to your mind. This is a good way to apply this tool to daily life. As we learn to follow Jesus more closely we will experience the rest, refreshment and blessings of His presence in our lives. To me, that seems to be a clear picture of what using the tool of fasting looks like.

Thank you, once again Mrs. Kempf.

Questions to Consider

- Is God leading your heart to a time of prayer and fasting in your life? What are some of the reasons that you would want to fast? Are you dealing with specific issues that only God can address?

- Proverbs 20:24 says, "How can we understand the road we travel? It is the Lord who directs our steps." Can we succeed without the wisdom of God? How could using the tool of fasting help us in understanding our life, what it is about, and where we are heading?

- We talked about keeping ourselves spiritually protected as we enter into fasting. Read Ephesians 6:10-18 referred to in the chapter. What is each item of protection that the Lord gives to put on, and what does each do?

- What encouragement does 1 Corinthians 10:13 also offer about our spiritual protection, whether we are fasting or not fasting?

- What are your thoughts about fasting? Has your view of using this tool in your life changed? Pick out ideas from this passage in the book of Isaiah 55:1-9. What should we be hungry and thirsty for? Is it the same list as you would have written? What are the blessings God is offering to us as we read this Scripture?

The Tool of Scripture

Psalm 63:1-5, Ezekiel 7:19-20, Zephaniah 1:5-7, Colossians 4:2, Jonah 2:2, Genesis 4:1-8,

Ephesians 3:18-19, 1 Corinthians 9:24-27, 1 Kings 3:5, Exodus 14:13-15, Proverbs 6:21

What's in My Toolbox

Afterwards

Are you ready to get to work? We have learned that God has equipped us with ten wonderful tools powerful enough to perform any task we are given. Each tool can now be placed in our Christian toolbox, prepared to go to work! Life has no guarantees, but we do stand a better chance of handling the hard trials with peace and confidence if we have built a foundation on Jesus. Our earthly journey is a process of progress and setbacks. By having the right tools, we can accomplish the job of working toward positive progress. I can not promise that the work will be easy or that there are no accidents waiting to happen, but I can promise that the benefits are of eternal proportion. We can live here on earth already knowing that we are citizens of heaven. Philippians 1:27: But whatever happens to me, you must live in a manner worthy of the Good News about Christ, as citizens of heaven.

We all need help; it has been my prayer that, by introducing these Christian tools, each one could be put to use and greatly aid us in completing the jobs we are each completing in our lives. The purpose of each principle was to support the message that whatever else we are doing, the work we are doing for the Lord is what matters most. These tools of the spirit are there to illuminate our vision, broaden our thinking and soften our hearts to the ways of God. Time away from God dulls our spiritual sensitivities. The further we move away, the easier it is to forget Him. It is our job to open up our toolbox and put to use the things that will sharpen our memory and build relationships. Turning our eyes to God's Word is what repairs the tears and snags our Christian journey sustains. By placing God's word as one of our core foundational pieces and yielding our ways to His ways, we allow God's work to happen in us. His work in us produces a godly life. See, there is always work to be done. It is because God is working inside us that we are prepared to be sent as His workers out into the world. Philippians 1:6 tells us, "And I am sure that God, who began a good work within you, will continue His work until it is finally finished on that day when Christ Jesus comes back again."

Tools sometimes are difficult to use, especially if it has been a while since we tried to make them work. If we don't consistently open our toolbox and keep the contents in good order, before long, dust settles and rust corrodes. I don't think I have to tell you that tools left to decay become ineffective and possibly dangerous when they are finally taken out again. It is the same with Christians. When we get lazy in our spiritual life, our attitude turns smug and self-satisfied. We foolishly say, "Everything is fine because I'm happy and comfortable." This leads us right into thinking too little of something too great, fueling our casual attitude towards God. Being involved with perfecting and using each tool allows us to remember God daily in times of both need and prosperity. Putting God first is the most important thing we can do; if all we do is focus on ourselves, we become misguided. 1 Kings

3:9 reads, "Give me an understanding mind so that I can... know the difference between right and wrong." Tenaciously seeking after God's wisdom is the only way that we can discern correct choices.

Each piece of our toolbox was studied from the prospective of seeking God's will and input above all else, so that, we do not fail to do what is right in God's eyes. In writing this discussion, it was my prayer to point out that there is no greater priority than loving and obeying God. Nothing else affects our eternal future so significantly. It will not be until we have intentionally grasped hold of the tools that have been divinely supplied for us and have aligned our priorities to God's standards that we live life to its full meaning. In closing, it is with anticipation of a much different today, a stronger tomorrow and blessed future that I challenge you to open your toolbox and take inventory of what's inside.

Through the Mother in Love Devotional Series, we have been searching the Scriptures and learning from other people's stories. Our mission is to be exposed to what a Christ-centered life looks like. After closing the lid on our now-filled toolbox, we have experienced the process of walking four steps so far. It helps to look back as our journey continues so we can rejoice in all the things that a relationship with Jesus has brought us. Book One taught us that we have fruit inside us waiting to grow. But nothing will grow if we do not invite the light of the Holy Spirit into our heart so it can shine on our potential and reap a harvest of abundance in our lives. Book Two established that, once the fruit is growing in our lives, we must remember where it began. The redeeming love of Jesus is what found us first; it is because of that love that we can return to Him. Book Three took us into the presence if God as we learned how to worship, praise and pray to our King. Praise and prayer could be the only next steps as we outwardly express what has been done for us on the inside. We were washed clean from sin and made free to bear the fruit Christ planted in each one of us.

We just completed Book Four, which emphasized that our relationship with Jesus should have always been one of continual growth and involvement. All the tools we researched put us in the position of having things expected of us. A Christian life is not one that takes but gives. This lifestyle is about being accountable to God here on earth through our behavior and priorities. No matter what step you are currently taking, our journey is about getting to our final destinations of moving towards God. Our sights must be set on maturing in our faith – start small and proceed ahead one day at a time. With the help of Christ in our life, there is no end to the maturing process. That is why I am so proud to say that I remain a work in progress! Will you commit to also being a work already begun that God is well pleased with? Will you avail yourself daily to every tool His hand has crafted? Ephesians 2:10 says, "He has created us anew in Christ Jesus, so that we can do the good things He planned for us long ago."

It is with humble gratitude for what God daily does in my life that I announce Book Five in the Mother in Love Devotional Series. The foundation has been laid. We have stepped to higher and higher heights with each level that our walk with the Lord has brought us to. If you have received Christ's love, are committed to His ways, praise His Holy name and use the recourses God provides, you are ready to celebrate the journey you are on! In fall 2010, you can begin to <u>Celebrate... Just Live It!</u> This will be the fifth step and the last volume in the Mother in Love Devotional Series. Join the celebration as we wrap up what a life well lived through the eyes of God looks like and the rewards that it promises.

Until then, be blessed.

About the Author

Mary's stories are taken from lessons she has been taught in life about the goodness of God. Her past struggles with an eating disorder inspired her to reach out with a message of hope that recovery is possible through faith. That time period of a personal battle brought about personal growth, physical healing and a new spiritual awareness. The life-changing experience that she and her family went through resulted in the blessing of starting her writing career. Mary published her first magazine article in April 2006 and published her first book in January 2008, titled, How a Mess Became A Message.

Her passion is speaking about what God can do in a life. Being an effective communicator of God's redeeming love is a privilege that she takes very seriously. Mary uses the Bible as a daily tool and applies its teachings to her life. She has studied the Bible in seminary level classes since 2001 and is currently attending the Hatfield Bible Seminary Leap Education program. Small group Bible studies also have been part of her background since 1993, providing her with the knowledge and Biblical understanding to write her devotions and reflective studies.

Mary married her husband, Tom, at the age of 19. Together they have been blessed with a son and two daughters. The Barrett family lives in North Wales, Pennsylvania. Some of the hobbies they enjoy together are camping in their RV, swimming, going to the beach and visiting loved ones.

Currently, Mary is involved in the "Mother in Love" conference series, based on her devotional books. She and her husband, Tom, are planting the seeds for a ministry they pray God will grow, named Titus II: 1 Ministries. Their vision is to bring together all who seek a relationship with Lord using a variety of outreach methods. Please feel invited to stay connected with the publications and speaking engagements at www.motherinlove.net.

Things To Work On